Sail-Railers

ROY POND

Sail-Railers

AN ALBATROSS BOOK

© Roy Pond 1992

Published in Australia and New Zealand by
Albatross Books Pty Ltd
PO Box 320, Sutherland
NSW 2232, Australia
in the United States of America by
Albatross Books
PO Box 131, Claremont
CA 91711, USA
and in the United Kingdom by
Lion Publishing plc
Peter's Way, Sandy Lane West
Littlemore, Oxford OX4 5HG, England

First edition 1992

This book is copyright. Apart from any fair dealing for the purposes of private study, research, criticism or review as permitted under the copyright Act, no part of this book may be reproduced by any process without the written permission of the publisher.

National Library of Australia
Cataloguing-in-Publication data

Pond, Roy
Sail-Railers

ISBN 0 86760 182 5 (Albatross)
ISBN 0 7459 2200 7 (Lion)

I.Title

A823.3

Cover illustration: Michael Mucci
Printed and bound by The Book Printer, Victoria

Contents

1	The Sail-Railer	7
2	Taste of adventure	17
3	The willy-willy	26
4	The prospector	36
5	Outback obstacles	43
6	The red pursuer	56
7	The camel lady	70
8	Tracking the past	82
9	Crisis of doubt	90
10	Boarding party	100
11	Fighting back	112
12	A cross marks the spot	119
13	An end to drifting	129
14	Camel route	140

1

The Sail-Railer

IT SAT ON A STRETCH of abandoned railway track in the middle of red, scrubby outback. It had a hopeful air as if waiting for a good push. 'This is it,' Michael said to Kirsty in a casual tone, trying to hide the shy pride he felt in his creation.

On the rusty rails stood a flat-topped trolley with a mast towards the front and at the rear a small wooden deckhouse to give shade and protection from the weather by means of canvas flaps that could be lowered at the sides.

They were standing in red dust under the shade of an umbrella mulga — Michael, Kirsty and an Aboriginal stockhand, named Maralinga Jim, who had helped Michael build the trolley.

Michael waited for exclamations of delight from Kirsty.

Praise, at least.

'So this is your secret dream,' she said eventually.

Michael's face darkened. She didn't like it. It just showed that you had to keep dreams to yourself. It was a mistake to share dreams.

Kirsty went closer, brushing some annoying flies away from her face, looking at the apparition on rails in disbelief. She gave a wheel of the trolley a kick with the toe of a sneaker, as if to test that it was real. Red rust smudged the toe of her sneaker.

'It looks like a billycart!'

He was bewildered by her response. How could she fail to admire it? He could think of nothing more satisfying than sitting on the trolley and rolling slowly along the section of abandoned rail line that ran through their cattle station property. It was a five kilometre stretch of track, overgrown with weeds. Once, it had linked the cattle station with the main line between Alice Springs in the heart of Australia and Adelaide in the south. The old main line had been ripped up long ago and the station's section of line now went nowhere.

'Billycarts don't have iron wheels like these and they can't go on rails,' he said, stung. They had taken the wheels from a crashed rail inspector's trolley, found lying beside the line — a pile of autumn iron that had turned red like the earth. The wheels and axles were the only things worth salvaging. They had scratched off the rust with steel wool. Most of it.

'Billycarts don't have a mast and sail, either,' Michael said, drawing her attention to the most remarkable feature of his craft. The mast, set into the deck and properly heeled for stability, was made from a wooden tent pole. The sail was an orange-coloured groundsheet secured at the top and bottom to spars. It was lowered rather than raised and it was sheeted to the deck with nylon ropes passing through metal eyelets. When they grew tired of pushing, it would be fun to let the wind carry them along the track.

It was Michael's favourite dream to sail away on the old line. In his imagination it was an endless stretch of track leading to boundless adventure.

'Yes, but where's the wind?' Kirsty said, throwing a bucket of cold reality over his dream. 'There hasn't been a whisper of wind since I've been here. I don't think the wind reaches Central Australia. It runs out of puff before it gets here.'

Michael looked at Maralinga. The Aboriginal scowled even more than usual. Maralinga had heavy brows, and eyes that looked as if they were set in deep disapproval beneath them, yet he liked Michael and he had enjoyed helping him build the trolley, even though it had meant working in his rest breaks, between jobs and after hours.

'Willy-willy come along pretty soon — blow this feller along,' Maralinga said defensively, referring to dry, twisting winds of dust that plucked at the red centre of Australia. He wanted to deflect the white girl's scorn.

Maralinga Jim resented the girl's presence, Michael thought. She was a stranger, a paying farm guest at the cattle station, along with her mother and father who were from England. She was staying in the visitors' lodge, a motel-style building adjacent to their wide-verandah farmhouse. Maralinga could not understand — even though times were tough — why cattle stations should become guest lodges for tourists who wanted a farm holiday in the Australian outback.

As if he expected a willy-willy at any minute, Maralinga turned and searched the flat, scrubby horizons. Michael and Kirsty followed his sweep of inspection. There was no sign of a willy-willy.

Not a leaf stirred on the umbrella mulga.

But Kirsty was wrong about there being no wind in the Centre, Michael thought. There were often good north-south winds. You only had to look at the alignment of the dunes to see proof of it. The winds just hadn't been blowing lately.

'Okay, so it's not a billy cart. Then I say it's a willy-willy cart!' Kirsty said, making a joke.

Michael was alarmed.

A joke about names at the unveiling of a new creation was risky. The name was likely to stick. He spoke up quickly. He wasn't going to have a farm guest tamper with his dream.

'It's the Sail-Railer,' he said.

'I think the Willy-Willy Cart sounds better.'

She was a girl who assumed a lot. She had followed Michael around the cattle station for days, showing a persistent though teasing interest in everything he did. She seemed intrigued by his air of secrecy. Finally he had given up trying to shake her off. Yet for Michael it had been a special concession to share this dream with an outsider, somebody who would leave forever, somebody who was not a part of his world. And now this... scorn.

'It's the Sail-Railer,' he said again, stubbornly. 'You can't go calling it a cart.' Secretly, he didn't mind the name Willy-Willy Cart. It sounded fun and quirky, like the willy-willy wind itself, but it lacked importance and a promise of great enterprise.

'Then how about the Willy-Willy Express?' she said.

He looked at Maralinga who shrugged.

'I'm sticking to the Sail-Railer,' Michael said flatly.

The laughter in Kirsty's taunting eyes and the smile on her wise, sisterly sort of face told him that she would never take the Sail-Railer seriously.

'Well, it will always be the Willy-Willy Express to me,' she said. 'I suppose we should launch her properly, though — break a bottle of Coke over her bow or something.'

'Too sticky. It'll bring ants.'

Maralinga licked his dry lips. 'I'll drink it first,' he said helpfully.

'No, thanks, this is a desert ship, so we can have a dry launching.'

'Go ahead, Michael — name her.'

'I just did.'

'I mean officially.'

'You want me to make a speech?'

'No, just name her.'

'I hereby name you Sail-Railer,' he said quickly.

'And may God bless all who sail in her!' Kirsty said in a posh-sounding English voice, like a member of royalty at a ship's launching.

'You sound like pommie prince feller,' Maralinga said, an impressed look on his face.

'Thanks, Maralinga. I suppose you mean a princess.'

'All aboard,' Michael said.

It was an exciting moment. The craft on the rails seemed alive and ready to go, rolling eagerly backwards and forwards as they clambered on board. Kirsty chose the shade of the deckhouse. 'You want me to sit here, don't you?' she said, assuming the deckhouse was meant for her.

'Wherever you like,' Michael said. There were places to sit in front of the sail or on either side of it. You could with some difficulty even sit on the roof of the deckhouse.

Michael stood up to lower the sail and secure it. The orange plastic sail cast a reflection of golden light over the deck. As luck would have it, there was no wind that day, not even a willy-willy. They waited. The afternoon sun stood over them, glaring like Maralinga.

Come on, wind, Michael willed silently.

They looked up at the orange groundsheet sail. It did not even stir. Michael licked a finger and held it up, checking for a breeze. He shook his head. Kirsty rocked her body back and forth like a child on a swing, hoping it would propel them along the rails. They did not move. The Sail-Railer was a prisoner of its rails.

Maralinga Jim gave a helpless shrug.

Michael wondered how they were going to make it go.

'We could try asking for wind,' Kirsty said.

'Asking who?'

'You know.'

Michael was a little shocked. 'You mean — ?'

'Yes.'

'I can't do that,' he said.

'Why not?'

'I'm not going to play games with him.'

'You mean it's your game and you're not letting him join in.'

'I didn't say that.'

'Do you think he only cares about our work and not the secret things we dream about? He may want us to travel along this track and if he does he'll help us. Go ahead, try asking.' She closed her eyes and folded her hands, as if the matter were decided.

Michael shrank from her suggestion. He gulped. Maralinga Jim quickly closed his eyes in case the girl picked on him next.

What was he supposed to say? His secret dream of sailing away on a lost railway line was suddenly becoming very public. He felt as if she were exposing it to the whole world — to the bush, the sky and the sun above. The universe was watching and listening.

Flies buzzed distractingly around his head.

Words wouldn't come. He didn't know what to say, especially in front of Kirsty and Maralinga.

He felt himself colouring. Kirsty would be disappointed in him and he hated the idea of failing in front of her. Kirsty opened one eye. 'Your eyes are still open,' she said patiently. 'Come on, we're waiting.'

He wouldn't. He'd refuse. This was his trolley and his dream and he didn't feel like revealing himself any more. The girl was trying to take over. 'You say something if you want to,' he said roughly.

She gave a sigh. 'All right, Michael.' She closed her eyes. Michael carried on watching her face as Kirsty's lips formed the words of a simple request.

'Father, give us the wind.' She said it in a voice filled with quiet assurance, then ruined it a bit by adding: 'Please.'

The bush held its breath. So did Michael.

He half-expected a gale to come roaring out of the flat, red scrubby earth that spread in every direction around them. Maralinga was also moved. He glanced hopefully at the sail. The orange plastic gave a single crackle of false hope. It was probably expanding in the heat.

The wind did not come.

2

Taste of adventure

WHERE WAS THE WIND? Michael thought.

So much for that.

'Our Sail-Railer isn't going anywhere,' Michael said, a bit relieved to end the experiment. 'Not without a push.'

'I give you kids a push,' Maralinga Jim said generously. 'You kids go flyin' alonga track.'

Maralinga went between the tracks and rested his hands on the back — big clever hands that were wonderful at metalwork and woodwork — and shoved. The Sail-Railer resisted only briefly, then began to roll, quickly gaining momentum. It was under way. Maralinga broke into a run, going over the rotting sleepers, between the lines.

Michael felt the vibrations of the wheels underneath them, bumping over joints in the rails.

He listened. The wheels sang an iron tune in a voice that was rusty from too little use.

'Here comes the wind!' Kirsty said. 'I can feel it blowing in my hair! I knew it would come!'

She cheered.

Maralinga tried to build up speed, but the sail met the rush of air in front. The sail braced itself to resist, sucking in its belly and slowing the trolley's progress like a parachute.

Maralinga stopped pushing.

'Get downa camp sheet,' he said.

Michael followed his instructions.

Without the drag of the large orange plastic rectangle, the Sail-Railer leapt ahead. 'Off you go — long ways,' Maralinga said. Maralinga gave them a hard push and let them go. They rode a good twenty metres before the wheels, squeaking in protest, stopped.

'Your wheels need a squirt of grease,' Kirsty informed Michael, 'but that was fun. Let's go some more. It's hot and I like feeling a breeze. It keeps these awful flies away.'

Maralinga caught up with them. Good-naturedly, he leaned against the Sail-Railer to push them again. He broke into a run and they soon reached a pleasing speed. Kirsty cheered. Michael softened towards her. Kirsty was finally appreciating his creation.

Then Maralinga lost his footing on a clump of weeds growing up between the tracks and fell sideways to the ground. Michael saw him drop from view. The Sail-Railer left his hands and went rolling on heedlessly without him, while Kirsty encouraged Maralinga with a stream of continuous praise and delight, not realising that they were travelling without power, her voice trailing behind the trolley like a vocal slipstream.

Maralinga sat in the dust chuckling.

'Come on, Maralinga. Push, push! I'm just starting to feel a breeze in my hair. This is fun! You can push us all the way to Alice Springs. . .'

The Sail-Railer had pretty good gliding power, Michael decided, as they trundled down the rails.

Kirsty's voice trailed off with the dying momentum of the trolley. She looked up at Michael. 'Why are we stopping?' She craned around the deckhouse and frowned to see Maralinga sitting on the ground, twenty-five metres away.

'Don't sit down on the job, Maralinga. Can't you push a couple of kids along? We're not heavy. Come back here and push us,' she said in a pretend-bossy voice.

She sounded even more like an English princess, Michael thought.

Maralinga shook his head. He stood up, still chuckling, and dusted himself off. He gave them a wave and went back towards the corrugated iron sheds. He was due back at work and risked trouble from Michael's father.

So did Michael. He was supposed to be baling hay for his father, using the baling machine.

But the launch of the Sail-Railer had been far more important.

He decided to stock the Sail-Railer with food, water, a sunhat and sunscreen lotion, everything he would need for an extended voyage into the outback. He had to be ready for the moment when the wind came up.

There were long silences at dinner that night.

His mother wasn't eating. His father, who normally developed a roaring appetite riding his motorbike around their 3 000 square kilometre property, picked around the edges of his plate.

'You didn't do much baling today,' his father said to Michael. 'I need your help in the school holidays. We need every bit of help we can get. You're not too young to know that times are very tough for us.'

'Sorry, Dad,' he said. He was only half listening. His mind was on the Sail-Railer. He pictured it sitting in the moonlight on its rusting rails. It called to him. He felt an urge to jump from the table and run to it — to sail away, even in the dark.

'If things don't improve soon we may be forced to sell up. We just can't find the money to keep things going.'

Michael had heard his father say this sort of thing a lot recently. It was something to do with repayments and banks and interest rates. Michael couldn't quite grasp how a single-storey bank building far away in Alice Springs could have any effect on their lives. But it seemed to bother his father.

'Things will get better, Dad,' he said.

'Sure, Mickey, if we find a gold mine on our property,' his father said with grim humour. 'How about Lasseter's lost gold reef? Maybe Lasseter strayed way off course and his lost gold reef is sitting out there.'

Every Australian school student knew about Harold Lasseter, especially Michael, who dreamed of stumbling on his legendary lost reef. It was said to be twenty-five kilometres long and three metres wide, running like yellow lightning through the outback about three hundred kilometres south-west of Alice Springs. The legend of Lasseter is probably the most famous lost treasure story in Australia. In an ill-fated expedition in 1931, Harold Lasseter had died in search of the reef he claimed to have discovered earlier, a golden reef hidden in the desert. It was worth sixty million pounds in Lasseter's day, or two billion dollars today. . .

'Don't,' his mother said, in a strained voice. She was near to crying. His mother was a strong-minded woman who could do things and who always coped in a quiet yet loving way. She disliked dreaming.

That was why he hadn't told her about the rail trolley. She wouldn't have approved. He hadn't told his father either, not because he wouldn't have approved, but because his father would then have known why Michael kept dodging the jobs he tried to give him.

He certainly wouldn't be telling him now.

If only the wind would come.

He lay in bed that night still dreaming of the Sail-Railer waiting for him on its stretch of track. He had walked the length of track many times and he knew every curve and feature. He had drawn a map of it.

He opened a bedside drawer and took the map out and examined it in the glow of his bedside lamp, following the Sail-Railer's route through the landscape of his memory.

Near the end of the track it passed a sharp, dog-faced projection of rock. Nearby there were old graves with crosses on top, memorials of the family who had first opened up the cattle station in the late 1800s.

Tracing the railway line with his finger, he followed it to its end. The tracks came to a sudden stop where two giant ghost gums stood like sentinels on either side of the track. The rails stuck out over the last sleepers like a fork over the edge of a table. He rolled up the map and put it under his pillow.

He switched off the bedside light. He closed his eyes and his mind went to the rails in the moonlight and he went along them, following them pleasurably to sleep.

That night he dreamt he was on Sail-Railer with Kirsty. Their sail was full of wind and they hurtled along the track across the plains. A willy-willy spun around the horizons of his dream.

Shrubs were bending, leaves clashing in the gum trees.

Michael slipped out of the baling shed. He

cast a glance towards the farmhouse to see if his mother was looking, then turned a hopeful look at the visitors' lodge to see if Kirsty was in sight.

He couldn't wait. He ran to the Sail-Railer.

'I hope you aren't planning to leave without me,' Kirsty said, appearing from behind a gum tree, holding a ribboned straw hat on her head. 'I'd hate to miss out on a journey with you. We're leaving for home the day after tomorrow.'

He felt a tug of emptiness like a small willy-willy swirling inside him. Kirsty was leaving.

This might be their last chance.

'Then hurry, let's go. There may not be another wind for days.'

They jumped on board the Sail-Railer. He let down the sail and sheeted it to the deck.

Kirsty noticed his bush hat, the canvas bags of provisions and the water bottles stashed in the deckhouse. 'I was right. You're all stocked up for a trip.' She scratched around in the bags and identified the contents. 'A cooking skillet, tin of ham, beans, oranges, water biscuits, shortbread fingers — yum. Your mother's going to get a shock when she goes to her pantry. Good, you've thought of everything, even a tube of sunscreen lotion.'

The orange plastic sail crackled and bellied

gently in the breeze. Disappointingly, it still wasn't enough to move them. Michael jumped out to give them a push to get started. It didn't take much to break the hold of inertia and the trolley trembled excitedly in his hands. He ran with it, pushing. Soon it was trying to pull away from him.

'Jump on board!' Kirsty said.

He ran around to the side and Kirsty grabbed his arm to help him on board.

They were off on the singing rails — under the power of the wind!

The wheels, freshly greased, squeaked softly like mice. The sail crackled and strained. The trolley trundled over the tracks. The scrub slid gloriously by.

Michael, unaccountably, felt tears sting his eyes. They were breaking free. Hope filled his heart like the wind filling the groundsheet. What could stop them now? What discovery awaited them at the end of their journey?

The dream soon ran out of puff. The breeze died and they stopped. But his heart was still beating wildly with excitement and he had a taste for the magic of motion aboard the Sail-Railer. They had run for at least a hundred metres before the wind died. . . the Sail-Railer had worked!

3
The willy-willy

THE WILLY-WILLY came out of the red, scrub-dotted outback like a spinning brown bush of dust, moving towards the rail line.

Kirsty screwed up her eyes in disbelief.

'Look underneath the willy-willy. There's a man walking in the middle of it.'

Michael followed her line of vision. She was right — or almost right. The man wasn't walking. He was dragging himself along with the help of a rough walking-stick made from a dried-up branch.

'He's limping,' Kirsty said. 'I think he's hurt.'

She climbed off the trolley and Michael followed. As they did so the willy-willy stopped moving, spinning on the spot, and the man stepped out of it towards them.

Then he dropped. It was as if the twisting force of the willy-willy had held him up until then and carried him along. Kirsty grabbed a water bottle from the deckhouse and followed Michael who went cautiously to the man.

He was lying on his back, his open eyes staring sightlessly at the sky. Michael stepped into the circle of the man's vision. The staring eyes were as blue as opals and his unshaven face as stubbly as the bush.

'You kids — here?' he said through cracked lips.

Kirsty knelt with the practised air of a nurse, lifted the man's head onto her lap and raised the bottle to his lips. He drank gratefully, but not overmuch.

'What are you doing on our property?' Michael asked, resentful of the man's unexpected appearance. He was spoiling things as well as trespassing.

'I wandered here. I do that a bit,' the man said.

He wore khaki bush clothes and a battered hat. He looked like an explorer.

'Who are you?' Kirsty said.

'Prospector.'

'You can't prospect here on our property.'

'I'm not. I'm on my way south.' He tried

to move and pain in his leg brought a grimace to his face. 'I've twisted my leg badly in a rabbit hole and can't walk any further.'

'Just great,' Michael said under his breath.

'Then come with us,' Kirsty said without hesitation. 'We'll put you on the trolley and push you back to the farmhouse.'

'No,' the stranger said. 'I'm going that way.' He pointed down the line in the opposite direction. 'I'll go with you on your rail car.'

'It won't get you far,' Michael told him. 'Our Sail-Railer only goes a few kilometres, then stops where the tracks end.'

The man's eyes looked disbelieving. He flicked a glance at the Sail-Railer as if it proved Michael wrong. Surely such a craft was built for a voyage, not to run up and down a piece of track, his expression seemed to say.

'Help me lift him,' Kirsty said.

They helped the man up and took his weight on either side. Michael picked up his stick. The stranger rested his arms on their shoulders and was able to hop along between them to the waiting trolley. The man's eyes examined the Sail-Railer like a pair of eager fossickers looking for gold.

'Who dreamed up this fantastic machine?'

'I did,' Michael said.

The prospector's eyes seized on Michael's face as if he had discovered a fleck of gold in a piece of quartz rock. 'You're a remarkable boy.'

They took the prospector to the edge of the rails and there he was able to swing himself on board and crawl into the shade of the deckhouse where his head and shoulders were protected.

'Who are you?' Michael said.

'Prospector.'

'Your name, I mean.'

'Jack. Jack Prospector.'

'That's handy seeing you are one,' Michael said sceptically.

Kirsty gave Michael a glare. 'I'm Kirsty and this is Michael,' she said, trying to make up for his rudeness.

'I'm sorry to break into your game,' the stranger replied. 'I suppose you were off on some adventure. I'm sure the last thing you wanted was a passenger.'

'We're glad we could help you,' Kirsty said.

'Maybe *you* are,' he said to her, then turned to Michael. 'But I don't think your friend here feels the same.'

Michael did not have a chance to answer.

Dust fingers tore at his hair and clothes and howled around the Sail-Railer, crackling and flapping the orange sail. Dust particles swirled around them. The willy-willy they had forgotten about had turned on them.

'We'd better hurry, Michael — let's start pushing him back.'

'I don't want to go back,' Michael said.

'You must come out of the wind,' the prospector told them. 'Climb on board.'

An urgency in his voice made them obey. Kirsty crawled partly into the deckhouse to escape it, but with her head sticking out so that she could watch the amazing storm spinning around them. Michael, afraid that the mast might be ripped out of the deck, held onto it.

The bush had vanished. A spinning wall of brown blocked it out. The spinning gained force, then suddenly it was calm. The wind no longer plucked at them, but tore around them in a circle. They had passed into the eye of the willy-willy.

Their trolley gave a lurch, the sail cracked taut and then they shot forward. They picked up speed. The mousey squeak of the wheels settled to a regular scurrying sound like rats' claws hurrying over metal. The rails sang.

Michael felt the suction of speed. He looked to either side. The twisting column of dust still blotted out his view. But they were moving fast, he could tell.

How long would it take to reach the end of the rails? Would they sail off the rails onto the hard-packed red earth? Would the Sail-Railer survive the crash?

He looked up at the straining sail, checked the tautly drawn ropes and swaying mast. Good old Maralinga. He'd made a good job of building her. The Sail-Railer could take it.

They ran on and on. For ages, it seemed. Was there no end to the rails? How long did it take to cover five kilometres? They must reach the end soon.

'I'm scared,' Kirsty shouted above the wind, holding onto her straw hat with one hand. The black ribbon on the hat flapped over her arm.

'Don't be frightened,' the prospector said calmly. He lay resting on his elbows, unafraid of the willy-willy's ripping force. The Sail-Railer ran recklessly on towards the end of the line.

'Hold tight,' Michael called out. 'We'll be reaching the end of the rails any minute.' Into his mind flashed a picture of the rails ahead, the place where two ghost gum trees flanked the line like sentinels and the severed rails stuck out past the sleepers like prongs of a fork over the edge of a table. They would career off the tracks and hit the earth.

'You mean we're going to fly off the rails?' Kirsty said. 'We're not going over a cliff I hope!'

'No, but we could be in for a bump.'

Dust still obscured his view. Surely they were at the end of the rails now? He thought he saw two tall shapes whip past the edges of his vision.

The ghost gums?

'Hold tight!' he shouted.

Michael waited for them to fly off the rails — waited for the bone-jarring crash.

It did not come.

They kept going. Were they running over desert? They couldn't be. There had been no bump. They were still running on the rails, the wind sweeping them smoothly along. They were in the power of something and careering headlong into the unknown.

Michael felt a shiver under his bush shirt. What should they do? Jump off? Did he really want to do that, just when the long-held dream was coming true, when his dream of sailing away to adventure was happening, when possibility was suddenly boundless — as boundless as it had always been in his dreams?

Michael had a sense of letting go and giving in to a force greater than himself. He became giddy and lay on the deck. His head was spinning like the willy-willy.

The swirling dust cleared, but the wind remained squarely behind them, filling their orange sail. They scurried along the tracks on a gentle downgrade across a red sandy plain in glaring sunshine and under a blue sky.

Kirsty and the prospector came out of the shade of the deckhouse to look. 'You know where we are,' Kirsty said, assuming Michael did.

Michael swept the terrain with a stare. All was flat. They were travelling south with the wind.

'Well?' she demanded.

Michael gave a helpless shrug. 'Don't ask me. There shouldn't be any track here any more. It was pulled up and sold in the eighties. The new line runs over a hundred kilometres away from here — in the west.'

'You're telling me we're travelling over tracks that don't exist?'

'Unless it's a section of track I didn't know about.'

'The tracks look real enough to me,' she said, 'even if they are rusty and overgrown. Maybe we should stop.'

'Why?'

'Before we go too far.'

The prospector lay in the deckhouse listening to them, his eyes flickering from one to the other as if trying to read their expressions. 'I don't think Michael wants to stop. This is his chance to go to the end of the line. You don't plan to stop, do you?' he said to Michael.

'No.'

'But where are we going?' Kirsty persisted.

'Wherever the wind takes us,' Michael said, shrugging. Couldn't she just ride along with it?

This was no time to start asking a lot of boring, sensible questions. Besides, there was something ahead on the line. It was a siding. Michael sat up. This would give them their first clue. It would tell them where they were on the map. . . *and in time*; at the back of his mind, a shivery idea had begun to grow. He had seen movies like *Back to the Future* where people had gone back in time. Was it happening to them now?

A rusting water tank and crumbling fettler's cottage, overgrown with weeds, slid into view. The siding hadn't heard the ring of wheels on its lines in over a decade. If they'd gone back in time, it wouldn't look like this. It would still be maintained. Michael relaxed.

But where were they? There was no name to be seen.

Kirsty looked around hopefully for signs of life as they rolled past the fettler's cottage; it lay deserted. She turned to the prospector. 'Do you know where we are?'

'We're on the old Ghan track, I'd say.'

'But Michael says it doesn't exist any more.'

'Michael knows differently. Do you think he built this fantastic machine to travel a few miles up and down a piece of track? No, he built it for a boundless voyage.'

Michael wasn't listening. His attention was fixed on the line ahead. Beyond the siding, the Sail-Railer came to a dried-up creek and a single span bridge. Michael looked at the rotting timber sleepers. Would they take the Sail-Railer's weight? They would soon find out.

The Sail-Railer reached the bridge, wheels squeaking faintly, and without slowing rolled out, high above the bone-white sand. The sound of the iron wheels changed to a hollow ring. Michael looked down at the creek bed fifty metres below them. A sleeper creaked. He saw a loose iron dog spike jump out as their wheels rattled a sleeper. It slipped between the gaps and fell to the sand far below. It looked very small when it hit the bed.

4

The prospector

THE WIND KEPT BLOWING. They careered across the open space, scarcely daring to breathe. Kirsty looked down and hid her eyes. The prospector smiled secretively.

Michael felt his hands go damp in spite of the dry heat of the day. He tried not to look down as they rumbled noisily over the bridge, but the drop below sucked his eyes to the edge. He looked down. The sandy bed far below exerted a pull — even on the Sail-Railer. He saw the railway lines bow under the weight.

For the first time, Michael tasted the metallic bitterness of fear in his mouth. Was the wind-force that had taken over their lives a kind force that wanted to thrill them, or a cruel force that wanted to destroy them? Perhaps these rails led not just to excitement, but to disaster.

He pulled his eyes away and looked ahead. If the old bridge suddenly gave in, they would die. The far end of the bridge seemed to take a step backwards with every metre they gained.

'Can I look yet?' Kirsty said.

'I wouldn't advise it.'

They sailed between two stretches of infinity, an endless blue sky above and an eternity below.

He felt his own body weight pressing on the deck of the Sail-Railer. He thought of Kirsty's weight, slender though she was, and of that of the prospector as he lay on his back on the deck, propped up on his elbows. Michael remembered the weight of the iron wheels and axles and the wooden deck. Perhaps the deckhouse had been a mistake. It was a stupid luxury, a bit of extra weight that could ruin everything.

He willed himself and the craft to be lighter. He pictured a giant hand cupping their craft, taking its weight and guiding them to the other side.

'You can look now.'

The sound of their wheels turned to a full, deep song of iron.

Kirsty looked back, appalled at where they had been.

Her eyes met Michael's and they seemed a little disappointed — as if he had betrayed her trust by putting her through such a scare. 'I went along with this game of yours, but I never knew you'd put me in danger,' her expression seemed to say. Michael flinched.

The Sail-Railer picked up pace, headed through lightly timbered country and over gentle undulations. Away to the left, a line of watercolour ranges was faintly visible. The bush slid past them at a satisfying speed. He was glad now that he had named her 'Sail-Railer' and not 'Willy-Willy Cart'. He'd been right. She was a ship of adventure, not a kid's toy.

The next grade was higher than the others. Michael wondered if the trolley would make it, but she built up enough momentum in the downgrade to fight her way to the top of it and, although they slowed, he did not have to get out and push.

'Look!' he said, pointing. Kirsty, who was scratching for something in the deckhouse, missed it. A frill-necked lizard, like a reptilian Tudor monarch, raced away from the rails, running on its back legs at blurring speed.

Kirsty came out and plonked Michael's bush hat on his head.

'What are you doing?'

'You've got to protect yourself from the sun,' she said. 'And you'll need some of this sunscreen lotion, too.' She took the cap off a tube of sunscreen lotion and sniffed it. 'This smells lovely, like a day at the beach.'

Trust a girl, he thought. He stuck out his hand. 'I can put it on myself, thanks.'

'Only trying to look after you.'

'Oh no,' he groaned silently. 'I've brought a little mother along.'

The Sail-Railer curved left and reached a downward gradient, gathering speed. Yet the freaky wind remained directly behind them, filling their sail. How was it possible? He did not even have to trim the sail.

They slowed as they approached some low hills, then headed down a grade again and out along a straight. They curved around a hill, down the side of another and then hit a patch of rolling sandhills.

A whining sound like that of a hornet floated on the breeze. The prospector came out of the deckhouse to look up. A small, silver, fixed-wing aircraft raced above the sandhills.

'They've come for me.'

The single-engined aircraft flashed overhead, so low that the wind from its passing buffeted their sail.

'What do you mean, come for you? Who are they?'

The aircraft banked and came back for another run, this time at an angle so that those inside could take a good look down at them. Michael saw men's faces pressed to the cockpit glass, tight faces, the eyes screened behind aviator sunglasses. Then they were gone.

They waited for the plane to come back, but the drone of the engine thinned out like a pencil line and the aircraft shrank to a full stop in the sky. It was gone and it did not come back.

The prospector gave a sad shake of his head.

'You can relax; they've gone,' Kirsty said. 'It doesn't look like they're coming back.'

'They'll come back. They always do. They've got our position now. They'll be back in something else — a four-wheel-drive, no doubt.'

'Why are they after you?' Michael said suspiciously. 'What have you done?' Anxiety tightened his voice. 'If you don't tell us the truth, we're not going to take you any further.'

'You'd throw me off? Just like that?' He studied Michael in wonder, as if finding an unexpected trace in a mineral rock sample.

'It's your choice.'

'You're the captain of this thing and your rules go, is that it?'

'That's it.'

'Don't listen to Michael,' Kirsty said, trying to smooth over the tension with a smile. 'We won't throw you off.'

'You may not, but Michael has his own ideas.'

'Let me handle this, Kirsty. It's my trolley. I'll decide who comes with us.'

'Very well,' the prospector said. 'I suppose I have no other choice but to take you into my confidence.'

'None,' Michael said.

The prospector shrugged. He unbuttoned a pocket in his trouser leg and pulled out a roll of paper. He opened it up. It was a map.

'Do you know what this is?' They stared at the map. It showed a railway line, and near one end there was a large cross.

'A map.'

'Not just any map.'

'Don't tell us — it's a *treasure* map.'

'You're very cynical for a boy who likes to dream. Or is it that you only have room for your own dreams? This,' he said, tapping the cross on the map with a square-tipped finger, 'is my treasure and I lost it many years ago. I'm going back to try to find the spot.'

'I don't believe it.'

'Why not?' Kirsty protested. 'That explains why those men are looking for him.'

'Good girl, Kirsty. I walked into a bush pub and, too trustingly, showed it to somebody, asking for help. Those men saw it. They've been following me ever since. They're greedy men who can think of nothing else but trying to steal my dream.'

'So why should we help you?' Michael said, his mind racing ahead. He thought of his mother and father and the problems they were having on the cattle station. Could this man lead him to treasure? He licked his lips. His throat was dry and he wanted a drink.

'Would you share your treasure with us if we took you there?'

The prospector's eyes gleamed as if he had discovered a promising rock sample after all. He laughed. 'Yes, Michael. That's the least I can do.'

5
Outback obstacles

'IT MUST BE VERY SATISFYING for you to have brought a dream like this to reality,' the prospector said about the Sail-Railer. 'She runs beautifully.'

'I'm satisfied.'

'I hope you don't mind if I get some shut-eye. I'm very tired.' The prospector yawned.

'You sleep,' Kirsty said to him soothingly and withdrew from the deckhouse. She crawled past Michael and went to sit at the front, ignoring him. He ignored her too, for a while, then crawled around the sail to join her at the front and sat beside her with the orange plastic sail at his back.

'I knew he was going to be trouble,' he said.

'The only trouble is your attitude to him. Don't you want to help people?'

'Of course I do. I let him come on the

Sail-Railer, didn't I?'

'I just hope you wouldn't rather have looked the other way.'

'I'd rather he hadn't been there. It's awkward and not the way I pictured things.'

'I know you're angry that he's joined us.'

'It's not him. I didn't want a grown-up along, looking over our shoulders, that's all.'

'It wasn't our choice. Something strange is happening to us. I don't understand what it is. Do you?'

He shrugged. 'What's there to understand? We're sailing away on an adventure.'

'Sailing where?'

'Somewhere, nowhere. Who cares? Let's wait and see.'

They watched the narrow-gauge lines snaking ahead of them. The converging lines twisted in the hazy afternoon heat. He was glad of the broad bush hat that protected his head and the sunscreen lotion that protected his body. He lowered his head to gaze dreamily down at the rails passing under the Sail-Railer. It wound in the track, kilometre after kilometre, like a reel.

'The line!' Kirsty suddenly shouted. 'There's a blockage on the line.'

Michael snapped out of his dream. A sand drift bulked in their path, completely covering the line. The rails vanished into a hill of red sand.

Derailment.

Michael clambered back to release the ropes that sheeted the sail to the deck, then hauled the sail up. The sail trolley slowed at once but continued to glide. They couldn't risk a derailment. If only Maralinga had built brakes.

He scuttled to the front again to join Kirsty, dropping beside her. He stretched out his legs, hoping to use them like buffers to cushion the impact. Kirsty did the same. 'Keep your knees bent and your legs up high so they don't get squashed,' he warned her.

Their feet hit the sandbank first, taking the shock of the impact. It did little to stop them. The force shoved their knees under their chins. The Sail-Railer gave a jump, but fell squarely back on the rails. Disaster had been averted.

'What's happened?' the prospector asked, sitting up. 'Have we hit the dirt?'

They had, literally.

'I hope you've got a shovel,' Kirsty said.

'I can't think of everything,' Michael said.

'Then what are we going to do?'

Michael thought about it. 'We're going to have to lift it off the rails and put it back on again on the other side of the drift.'

'Sounds sensible. Can we do it?'

'Maralinga and I lifted it. We'll have to try.'

The prospector sat up. 'I'll give you a hand.'

He dragged himself out of the deckhouse and swung first his good leg then the sprained leg over the side. Kirsty gave Michael a prodding look and he climbed off the trolley to help, allowing the prospector to rest one hand on his shoulder as he straightened himself. The prospector winced a bit, but straightened. 'My leg's almost as good as gold. It's already feeling better for the rest.' He stood at the side of the rails, holding onto the trolley.

Michael walked around the sand drift to evaluate the situation. The red sand drift covered the tracks for a distance of about five metres. He came to a decision.

'Perhaps the easiest thing would be to go straight over the top,' he said. 'We'll have to roll it over the sand together. Think you can help?' he asked the prospector.

'I'll give it a go.'

'We'll work from the sides. You and Kirsty grab it and push on this side. I'll go to the other side.'

They pulled the trolley back to give it a bit of a run then rolled it forward. The wheels hit the sandbank, slowed, the iron wheels sinking in gritty sand but still rolling. The Sail-Railer climbed. It was working. 'Keep it straight,' Michael instructed them. 'Don't let it slide off to one side.'

A fear tapped on the back door of Michael's mind and gave new energy to his efforts. What if the men chasing the prospector came now — while the Sail-Railer was stuck like a fish on the shore? What would the pursuers do to the prospector — and to them?

'We're getting there,' the prospector said. 'Not far to go now.'

Michael pushed harder. The trolley's wheels bit into the sand. The Sail-Railer was solid, despite Maralinga's efforts to keep weight to a minimum. Yet between them, he and Maralinga had lifted it onto the rails once before. He recalled the wiry strength of the Aboriginal stockman and felt new respect.

The Sail-Railer's wheels stopped, hopelessly held by the red sand.

Michael went up the sandbank surefootedly, like a camel on a dune. He stopped at the crest. How much further did the Sail-Railer have to go before it met the rails on the other side? He measured the distance with a glance. Only a couple of metres to go and the Sail-Railer would be over the hump and could run easily down the other side to rejoin the rails — if only they could budge it.

But the wheels had sunk into the sand almost to the axles. Michael rubbed his chin. What should they do? Roll it back and try something else? He felt exposed on the sand hill as if the sky were watching. It reminded him of a scary TV documentary he had seen about new-born turtles fighting for survival on a beach. They were trying to crawl to the safety of the sea under the wheeling shadows of seabirds who attacked like dive bombers.

A memory came back of the silver aircraft that had raced over the sandhills and flashed overhead, so low that the wind from its passing had buffeted their sail; how it came back for another run, this time at an angle so that those inside could take a good look down at them; he had seen men's faces pressed to the cockpit glass, tight faces, the eyes screened behind aviator sunglasses.

'They'll be back. They always do. They've got our position now. They'll be back in something else, a four-wheel-drive, no doubt.'

There was one possibility. He could slide something under the front wheels so they wouldn't dig in deeper. A couple of flat stones might do it. He went over the top of the mound and slid down the steepness of the other side, riding the sand like a skateboard with the soles of his sneakers. Dust billowed around him. He hit firm ground and stamped the red dust off his feet.

A patch of saltbush looked promising. He went into it, looking for loose stones. He spotted some flat, weather-scrubbed stones nestling against saltbushes. They would do. He crouched, lifting a stone, letting daylight flood into what until that moment had been a secret, dark place. The scorpion underneath sprang like a released spring at Michael, its barbed tail stabbing the air.

Michael fell back with a cry of alarm and disgust, the stone still in his hands. He got up, shaky inside and angry, even though it had missed him. It had come loathesomely close. He wanted to drop the stone on the scorpion's metallic head and squash it flat, but something stopped him. The scorpion danced to face him, squaring up to him like a fighter in a ring, occupying the smooth hollow left by the stone. 'Sorry,' Michael said to it. 'I'd also be mad if somebody ripped the lid off my home. I'll let you go, but I need your roof.'

'Hurry up,' Kirsty said.

He carried the stone back to the sand drift

and went back for another. He was more careful this time, kicking the stone over with the toe of his sneaker to check underneath before picking it up.

He laid the stones in front of the wheels, bedding them down so that they made a rise, but not enough to obstruct the wheels like chocks.

'Let's try again,' he said. It worked. They pulled it back a bit then made a run. The Sail-Railer's front wheels hit the stones and rose. They pushed harder and she climbed to the top of the mound.

'Slowly,' Michael cautioned. 'Don't let her roll down the other side.'

The sand drift obscured the rails for some distance after the mound. Where exactly did the rails begin? He had to be sure.

'Hold her steady,' he said. He let go of the Sail-Railer and went down the other side again.

He followed the sand to where the rails reappeared and squatted down on his haunches. He smoothed the hot sand around the rails so that only the tops of the rails peeped out. There was a magic about things half-hidden, he thought. He loved the look of the brown ribbons of iron just emerging through the red sand. He tried to run the flat of his hand over the rail like a grader, pushing sand aside and revealing the length of line. It was like putting his hand onto the hotplate of a stove. 'Ouch!' He jumped. Too hot. What a pity. It would be soothing to smooth the sand over the rails.

'Stop playing, Michael!' Kirsty said.

He straightened reluctantly and looked at his handiwork, turning his head on one side to appreciate the effect of the two brown lines splitting the red sand. That should help. He rejoined the others at the top of the mound. The prospector looked amused.

Kirsty shook her head. 'He's like a kid in a sandpit.'

They pushed the Sail-Railer over the crest of the mound. It seemed eager to rejoin the rails, pulling towards them. They couldn't hold it. 'Meet the rails, meet the rails,' he willed it and it almost did. Then it slid and landed heavily, one wheel resting on the outside of the rail and the other on the inside, sunk in the sand he had smoothed with his hand.

'It's time to do some weight-lifting,' he said, wishing Maralinga were with them.

They took hold of the base of the trolley and strained. It lifted a few centimetres, but not enough to go back on the rails. They let go, resting to get their breath back. Why couldn't they lift it? It had gained weight since Maralinga and Michael had wrestled it onto the tracks.

He remembered the provisions on board. The bottles of water, the food — he would have to take them out and lighten the load before they could lift it. 'I'll have to do some unpacking.'

He went aboard and came out with water bottles and canvas bags filled with provisions, including heavy cans. He put them on the ground beside the track.

They tried again. They strained. This time the wheels rose level with the top of the rails, but the prospector lost his footing and collapsed on top of the trolley.

'Sorry, crew.'

That's when Michael saw the spangle of sunlight on a windscreen in the distance. A four-wheel-drive vehicle was bounding across the sandhills towards them, dust fanning out behind it.

'When I say three — lift. One, two, okay — lift.'

'You didn't say three,' Kirsty complained, letting go.

'We've got to move quickly,' Michael said. 'There's a car coming.'

They looked. In the distance a red Land

Cruiser bounded over the crest of a sandhill and half-slid down the slope, like a beetle.

'One, two, three,' Michael said.

The threat of the approaching Land Cruiser gave new strength and focus to their efforts. They strained muscles and sinews and this time the wheels lifted clear of the lines. 'Sideways a bit,' Michael instructed them. It was directly above the rails and ready to be let down. 'Easy, now, let her down.'

The Sail-Railer landed firmly back on the rails.

'I'll spread the sail and we'll run for it,' he said. 'Climb on board,' he called to the prospector. 'Kirsty, help me give her a good push, then jump on board.' He lowered the sail while the prospector craned anxiously around the deckhouse to check on the progress of the red Land Cruiser. It was putting on a spurt of speed. Sand billowed out behind it like a brown parachute.

The prospector helped Michael sheet the sail down securely. Michael jumped out to help Kirsty push. They leaned against the Sail-Railer. It began to roll.

'Our food and water!' Kirsty said, twisting to look back.

'Too late!'

'We can't go without water,' Kirsty said, letting go and running back around the sand drift.

Now the wind filled the sails of the Sail-Railer and it tugged against Michael's hands. What should he do? Take the sail up again? He checked on the Land Cruiser. It was a few kilometres away and closing fast. Releasing the sail and letting it up would lose them time.

'Hurry, Kirsty! I can't hold it back!'

'Shall I take up the sail?' the prospector said.

'No!'

Kirsty darted back to the little stack of provisions sitting beside the rails in the soft sand. She grabbed a canvas bag at random and two water bottles.

The wind trolley was straining against Michael's arms now, like a big hound eager to run. To hold it, Michael dug his heels into a rotting sleeper. A piece broke off and the rest powdered underneath his foot. He let himself be dragged to the next one. It crumbled, too. He fell, almost letting go, but held on with one hand. The Sail-Railer took off, dragging him bodily over the bumpy sleepers. He got back to his feet, a hand-grasp away from disaster. The prospector looked helpless.

Kirsty was running to catch up. Michael tried to brake the trolley's run with his heels. He couldn't stop it now, but he could slow it. Thump — his heels hit another sleeper. He slid off it to the next. Kirsty was almost at his shoulder, running, the bag and bottles filling her arms. He could hear her whimpering with effort.

The Sail-Railer gave a shiver under Michael's hand. A strong gust bellied the sail and its timbers creaked with the strain of being held. Kirsty was running level with him now. She pulled ahead. She stumbled, but kept going. A water bottle flew out of her hands and thudded heavily beside the rail line. Michael thought of taking his hands off the Sail-Railer and making a grab for it, but he couldn't risk it. The Sail-Railer was going too fast and would break away.

The prospector leaned over the side, his arm outstretched. She handed him the remaining water bottle, then the canvas bag.

The prospector took them. She held out her hand for the man to help her on board. He shook his head.

Why didn't he put out his hand to help her? Was the prospector going to leave her? The trolley tried to rip itself out of Michael's hands.

Did the prospector want to leave them both behind in his anxiety to escape the pursuers?

6
The red pursuer

THE PROSPECTOR DRAGGED his legs over the side of the Sail-Railer and sat on the edge. He was blocking the way. She couldn't get past him to climb on board.

'Help me!'

'Dive.' He put out his arms. Kirsty launched herself. The prospector's arms closed around her and he rolled with her, taking her safely onto the deck.

There was no time for Michael to run to the side. He dived at the trolley, clinging to the roof with his fingers. He found a toehold in the decking, and raised himself onto the roof where he sat, panting, his head turned back to check on the advancing Land Cruiser.

Kirsty raised her head above the deckhouse roof to look anxiously back in the same direction. 'Can we get away?'

'We can try. Keep low,' Michael said.

'Why? Do you think they have a gun?'

'Maybe not, but we mustn't take a chance.'

She ducked down and joined him under the roof; they flattened themselves to the floor and peered out apprehensively.

The Sail-Railer gathered speed on the rails. Their orange sail bellied in the wind, straining against the spars and ropes. Red sandhills whipped past. The wheels underneath them ran with a steady, clear ring on the tracks.

Go Sail-Railer, Michael thought. The Sail-Railer was going to give them a run. He raised a finger to the Land Cruiser in a rude gesture as it beetled over the searing ridges. The driver was probably too far away to see Michael's action, but it made Michael feel better.

The Sail-Railer was going well, but there was one problem. However well the Sail-Railer ran, a wind trolley was never going to outrun a Land Cruiser. It was just a matter of time before the gap closed and the Land Cruiser caught them.

How could they escape it? They needed to reach a bridge or a cutting, a narrow pass where only the Sail-Railer could go, Michael thought, as long as the sides of the pass weren't too high or they might rip off their sail.

He searched the converging rails ahead, but there was no promise of an escape. They blew into another ruined siding. He glimpsed a blurr of ruined stone buildings, a pumper's hut, abandoned fettlers' quarters, a rusting overhead tank. They rattled through the siding, going along the length of a cracked, overgrown platform.

The ruins acted as a windbreak and slowed their progress. They did not regain full speed until they had rolled thirty metres beyond the siding.

Where was the red Land Cruiser? Michael had lost sight of it behind the buildings. He looked up at the mid-afternoon sky. There'd be several hours of sunlight before the light went.

They regained full speed, tipping down a gradient. A range of flat-topped hills rose on their left. One of them had a cup-shaped peak. They curved right and ran towards a narrow cutting in a hill. Would it be narrow enough to block the red Land Cruiser?

They passed through it, narrowly clearing the sides. Michael and Kirsty looked back. The Land Cruiser slowed when it reached the cutting but, to their disappointment, it worked its way through.

'Great,' Michael said, with hopeless sarcasm. What was going to save them? Were they going to be caught so easily?

Hope came around the next bend. They reached the course of a dried-up creek with steep sides that fell away. A narrow, rotting bridge with dangling sleepers stretched across it. Michael again raised a jubilant finger to their pursuers who by now were close enough to see.

The Sail-Railer ran out over a hundred metre drop. The rusted bridge, although made of girders, with latticed sides, swayed drunkenly like a rope bridge, but they kept going. Until, that is, they hit a barrier.

The dried-up water course, which in flood carried a torrent of water, also channelled an invisible river of air. It hit them from the side, deflecting the wind behind them and making their plastic sail flap in confusion. The Sail-Railer came to a squeaking halt, perched high above the bleached sand of the riverbed.

Michael looked despairingly at the sail. It flapped as uselessly as a wet sheet on a washing line. He would have to trim it. The wind was coming from a new angle. He reached for a rope to release the sail. A sleeper underneath the trolley complained. A rotting sleeper gave a loud crack like a pistol shot. The Sail-Railer shuddered. Kirsty gave a strangled squeak, as though afraid that a good scream might bring the whole thing down.

They waited for the bridge to go. The trolley would plummet like an elevator with a broken cable, Michael thought and, with their combined weights on board, it was probably just as heavy as one, but there would be no automatic brake system to slow them, no buffers to cushion their fall, just a free fall to oblivion on the river bed below.

The Sail-Railer steadied and the bridge held.

Gingerly, Michael undid the ropes securing the sail to the deck. He changed the angle of the sail and secured the ropes. The sail filled and strained against its ropes. But the Sail-Railer quibbled with the wind, resisting like a reluctant dog on a lead. The mast squeaked in the deck. The trolley shook itself. Don't do that, Michael told it silently. Don't you dare.

It obeyed him. They moved on. Kirsty didn't dare cheer. They crawled across the void.

They were halfway across. They heard the roar of an engine. The Land Cruiser's bonnet and bull-bars loomed on the edge of the chasm.

It lurched to a stop with a squeal of brakes, its long whip aerial quivering. Two men jumped out and ran to the bridge.

'We've got to go faster. I'll have to get out and push us,' Michael said.

'No, Michael, the sleepers are rotten. You'll go right through them.'

'Don't worry, I'll be careful. I've seen the drop below.'

Michael slid his legs off the trolley and felt with his foot for a secure sleeper. He met something that gave like papier-mâché. It squeaked under his sneaker, but it seemed able to take his weight. Keeping one hand on the trolley to save himself if it broke, Michael put his full weight on the sleeper. He leaned against the trolley and pushed.

'They're coming onto the bridge!' Kirsty whispered.

The prospector shook his head sadly. 'Is there no stopping their greed?'

Michael pushed harder. He stepped onto the next sleeper. It crumbled under his heel, but he kept his foothold and kept pushing. The Sail-Railer rolled on. The sail gave a strong tug.

Michael dared a glance over his shoulder. A large man dressed in a safari suit and wearing dark glasses stepped out exploratively onto a sleeper. When it held him, he took another step and then, more confidently, a third. The second man, following at his shoulder, urged him on. With his fourth step the man nearly took a journey to the riverbed, as a sleeper disappeared with a crack under his weight. He fell heavily between the rails, his arms hooking around them, his sunglasses slipping askew on his face. The other man backed off.

'Help me,' the hanging man yelled.

'You want us both to go over?'

Michael gave a loud laugh and Kirsty a whoop of delight. They widened the gap between themselves and their pursuers.

The man hanging on the rails lifted himself like a gymnast on parallel bars, but he was in no hurry to go further. He picked his way gingerly back to the edge.

On the last stretch of the bridge, the wind changed quarter again, blowing from directly behind them. Michael climbed back on board and set the sail squarely. The Sail-Railer galloped to the far side.

A burnt red sunset settled like darkening coals over the hills to their right. They did not stop. They needed to put as much distance between themselves and their pursuers as they could.

The sunset died and the stars came out over the outback, chips of glitter-bright light on a midnight-blue sky. A nearly full moon hung suspended among them, casting an eerie light on the passing scrub. With the sun gone, the dew settled and the temperature dropped.

'Shall we stop for the night?' Kirsty suggested.

'If we do, we'll make it easier for them to round us up in the morning,' the prospector said. 'I say we just ride on.'

'But what if the rails end or there's another sand drift or a rock-slide or a broken bridge?' Kirsty asked.

'Our luck's got us this far. It'll keep us going,' Michael said.

'You really think it's luck?' the prospector said.

What else? Michael thought.

They travelled on under the stars — stars that looked down on real ships at sea. What did the stars make of their Sail-Railer scuttling over the tracks? Michael wondered. Had a craft as strange as this ever voyaged across Australia before?

'I'm getting hungry and chilly,' Kirsty said. 'Can't we stop now and make a little fire and have a break?'

'I think it'll be safe now,' the prospector said, giving them permission. 'But only for a short break.'

Michael felt a twinge of irritation. It was Michael's Sail-Railer and as the captain it was his place to decide when they stopped. They should ask him first, he thought resentfully.

Kirsty did. 'Aren't you going to stop here, Michael?'

'Okay.' He undid the ropes and took up the sail and they slowed. They climbed off the trolley ahead of the prospector and helped him onto the side of the tracks.

They stretched their legs. It was a wonderful feeling, like a tickling deep in the bones. Michael reached inside the deckhouse and took out a canvas bag, the water bottle and a knife in a sheath.

He had no difficulty finding wood for a fire. He hacked off slices of dried, rotting sleeper — although careful to choose sleepers behind the trolley — and made a pile beside the track. He produced a box of matches from the canvas bag and lit a few shavings for tinder. The tinder gulped flames into itself and the flames spread to the wood. They were soon cheered by the warm glow of a fire, their nostrils filled with the smell of burning wood.

The smell made Michael think of food. Hunger made an empty space inside him as big as the night sky. He needed to fill it, quickly. He found a can of ham and beans — borrowed from his mother's pantry — and a small camp skillet with wire handles that opened from the sides. He chopped up the ham and stirred it in with the beans.

'I'm glad we brought him,' the prospector said.

'You don't have to cook and do everything,' Kirsty said to Michael, softening. 'I'm not one of those bossy girls who refuses to do anything her mother used to do just to show she's equal.'

'It's okay,' he said. 'I'm not one of those boys who wait for a girl to do everything.'

The ham and beans bubbled and gave off a pleasing aroma.

'Sorry I haven't got plates — just two spoons and a fork, that's all — so we'll have to eat out of the pan. Just dig in.' They dipped their implements hungrily into slightly seared ham and beans.

'Magnificent,' the prospector said. 'I don't reckon they ate this well in the dining car aboard the old Ghan that used to run on these tracks — mind you, some say the old train still does make an appearance now and then.' He paused as he swallowed a mouthful of beans and ham and looked unsure about whether to continue. Michael's interest sharpened. Kirsty stopped chewing.

'You mean a ghost train?'

'The Ghost Ghan. I've met old bushies who say they've seen it come thundering out of the darkness on a moonlit night, streaming shreds of steam like mist. They hear the scream of its steam whistle.'

'When did the real Ghan run?' Kirsty said, trying to switch tracks in the conversation and lead it in a less disturbing direction.

'The old Ghan hasn't run since 1980. It started running in the late 1920s, ending the isolation of Central Australia. Until then, Afghan cameleers were the only link between South Australia and the Centre. Great camel trains used to traverse thousands of kilometres of wilderness to bring essential supplies to those in the red heart. That's where the Ghan train got its name. It's short for *Afghan*.'

'It's no surprise that bushies have seen it,' Michael said a bit scornfully. 'It still operates. The old Ghan steam train runs on a thirty-five kilometre stretch of restored track just outside Alice Springs. I've been on it,' he added, caught up in the conversation in spite of the reserve he felt towards the stranger.

'I'm talking about here.'

'The Ghost Ghan, here? You mean it might come thundering out of the darkness at us after all?' Kirsty said. She shivered.

'Getting cold?' the prospector said.

'Getting scared.'

Michael threw some more pieces of rotting sleeper on the fire and she edged a bit closer to him. 'You don't believe in ghosts, do you?' she asked the stranger.

'Believe in them? I don't put my faith in them, if that's what you mean,' he said, avoiding her question.

'How did you get to be stumbling through the desert with a twisted leg?' Michael asked, taking the relaxed mood as an opportunity to find out more about their mysterious passenger. 'If you really are a prospector, where's your metal detector?'

'Michael,' Kirsty said warningly.

'No, let him. I know I bother him. But I can't answer your questions, Michael. A lot of things are a mystery and must remain so.'

'Will you tell us a bit more about your treasure? What is it? A gold reef, like Lasseter's?'

The prospector's face, lit by the firelight, took

on a melancholy glow. 'Lasseter, ah yes. Like others, he died out here. Some say he still goes looking for his lost reef.'

'The ghost of Lasseter?'

'Some say.'

Michael and Kirsty exchanged uneasy looks. Michael edged a little closer to Kirsty.

'Who are you, really?' Michael said. The firelight found an answering glow in the eyes of the prospector. But it revealed nothing and neither did the prospector.

'I'm Jack Prospector.'

'That's not a real name. It's a made-up name. What do you really do?'

'I prospect. I search or explore for valuable finds.'

'Like gold?'

'Like gold. I had a piece of gold I kept in a pickle jar. A big, flat nugget the size of a baby's hand. The men who've been chasing me stole it. But they want more.'

'And you're going to share your secret with us? You won't try to trick us?'

'I'll happily share my secret — and sorrow — with you.'

A dingo out in the darkness gave a desolate cry.

'What was that?' exclaimed Kirsty.

'Just a dingo's call,' the prospector said.

'I think we'd better go on,' Michael said. He washed out the skillet in coarse sand and scraped it clean, then stamped out the fire.

They drank some of the water from the water bottle, limiting themselves to two mouthfuls each.

Once more, they boarded the Sail-Railer.

7

The camel lady

MICHAEL WAS GLAD OF THE BREAK, but it was good to be on the move again, even in the dark. He expected the bright headlights of the Land Cruiser to spill across the hills at any moment. How much time had they gained? The sheer creek bed would have forced the pursuers to drive around the dried-up water course in search of a way across?

Would they push on across open bush at night, risking a broken axle or a ripped tyre — or worse? Maybe they would be sensible and camp for the night, confident that with their superior speed they could overhaul the trolley the next day.

The orange sail, a pale square above his head, filled with wind and swept them along the tracks. He marvelled at the wind. How could it always sit behind them, so reliable and constant?

Noises increased in the darkness. The iron wheels squeaked more loudly than he remembered in the daylight and clicked firmly over the rail joints. The moonlit bush slid palely past. They grew drowsy and decided to rest. They found two blankets. The prospector took shelter in the deckhouse, lowering the canvas flaps to shield himself from the cold. Kirsty and Michael took the blankets and curled up on the deck, pulling their hats low over their faces for extra warmth.

From where he lay, Michael could see the track stretching away into the darkness. He tried to stay awake to watch the track ahead, but soon dozed.

He dreamt he was on a rail trolley, powered by the wind, running over the Australian outback in the dark. Stupid dream. He woke up with a jolt. It was stupid all right, but it was also true. They were running in the dark. Who was watching? Who was in control? He looked at Kirsty. She lay asleep on the deck. He looked into the shadows of the deckhouse. He'd be asleep, too.

He must keep watch. They all depended on him. The wind had died a little and they ran at a gentle, steady clip. He looked at his wristwatch. The luminous hands told him it was nearly midnight.

He thought of the Ghost Ghan. What would he do if he heard the shriek of a steam whistle and the hissing clamour of a locomotive?

It was easy to believe that on a moonlit night like this it could come scouring out of the night at them, streaming shreds of steam like mist. What happened when a ghost train hit you? Did it blast right through your body? Would it smash them to pieces?

Forget ghost trains, he told himself sternly. There were enough scary things happening.

Like the appearance of the man whose legs lay stretched out beside him.

He made a simple connection in his mind. Ghost Ghan, ghost prospector. If he could believe in one, why not the other?

What if he didn't really exist at all? What if their mysterious hitchhiker were none other than the ghost of Lasseter, stalking the outback in search of his treasure? But why here? If it were Lasseter, he had strayed many hundreds of kilometres off course. Did ghosts make errors?

The prospector gave a grunt in his sleep, snoring softly. Did ghosts snore? The sound was reassuring.

Michael swallowed and turned his eyes away. So maybe he wasn't a ghost. But was he for real? Was his story about a treasure map true? And were the strangers who were following him doing so for the reasons he claimed?

Michael drifted back to sleep, listening to the song of the wheels and the clickety-clunk as it went over joints. He heard dingoes crying far off, but they could not call him from sleep. His wind trolley carried him further and further through the landscape of his dreams.

Michael woke up, the morning sun shooting lances of light into his eyes. They were trundling over flat gibber country. The wind must have blown all night. It was a desert landscape littered with millions of naked-looking stones, scattered as far as the eye could see and stripped bare of sand by the wind. It looked as if a hailstorm of meteorites had hit the plain. It was true what many visitors to the outback said. Central Australia was the closest thing to being on another planet he thought, stretching.

Kirsty was still asleep, curled up in a blanket, her head resting on an arm, the brim of her straw hat making a roof that hid her face in shadow.

The first rays of light probed under the brim. She looked very content and justified in her sleep as if this mad adventure only went to prove something she'd said.

Michael sat up and peered into the deeper shadow of the deckhouse where the prospector lay. He could just make out the man's face. It was a sharp face, with a probing look to it like a miner's pick. What had brought him into their lives? Michael wondered if he had a wife and children of his own waiting somewhere.

He looked back at Kirsty. She opened one brown eye and smiled at him. 'You've been staring. How long have you been doing it? That's not fair. I suppose I look groggy.'

'Morning, crew,' the prospector said, sitting up.

'Morning,' Kirsty said through a yawn. 'How are you feeling?'

'I could do with a coffee and a morning paper,' he said cheerily. He was trying to put them at ease, to make up for his frightening ghost stories of the night before, Michael thought.

'Coffee! Don't mention liquid,' Kirsty said. 'I could drink our water bottle dry.'

Michael swallowed drily. There were a few oranges in the canvas bag. He fished them out and cut them into quarters, using his sheath knife. He handed them around. In the dry desert air, the acid perfume of the fruit pricked their nostrils and Michael's mouth watered. He was thirsty and hungry. He bit hungrily on an orange quarter and allowed the juice to wash down his throat. Kirsty and the prospector did the same.

Michael dipped again in the canvas bag and produced some shortbread biscuits. They ate one each and it cheered them. 'We've got to find some water,' Michael said.

They found more water than they needed. Or so it appeared at first.

It was around midday. The Sail-Railer slowed, battling a gradient, came over the rise and went rumbling down into a plain filled with shimmering water that made them narrow their eyes against the glare.

'Flood!' Where had the water come from? The gibber country was drier than blotting paper.

They were heading straight into it. They couldn't stop in time. The Sail-Railer ploughed into the shimmering plain. But there was no water there — and no wind, either!

The Sail-Railer rolled to a halt, not a breath of air in her sail. They were marooned in a sea of searing heat and reflections.

'We could die here,' Kirsty said after an hour had passed without the wind returning.

'Don't be dumb. The wind'll come up again.'

'You have a lot of faith in the wind,' the prospector said, 'but not in much else. Why is that?'

'Because it was his idea to sail away on this silly, willy-willy machine. It's his game, so he believes in it.' She knew an awful lot about him for a girl who had only known him for eleven days, Michael thought resentfully.

'Do you only believe in your own dreams, Michael? I get the feeling you don't believe in mine.'

'I never said that,' he protested.

The prospector looked at him keenly. 'How different you are from Kirsty. She believes in other people's dreams and is willing to go along with them.'

'Maybe she doesn't have dreams of her own,' Michael said. Kirsty's eyes flicked away. She was hurt by the remark.

'Do you have dreams, Kirsty?' the prospector asked. He liked to dig away at people. Maybe the man really was a prospector after all, Michael thought acidly.

She shrugged. 'Not lonely ones. I always dream of sharing a dream.'

'Then you're a lot wiser than both of us,' the prospector said.

Michael's faith in the wind and in his own dream did not help. The wind did not come.

Thirst shrivelled their throats. Michael thought of pushing the Sail-Railer across the plain. But the effort would only make him thirstier. Shimmering heat waves lapped against the rails. He felt he could dive off the Sail-Railer and go down into cool depths below the gibber plain.

They allowed themselves another mouthful of water, then they crawled under the canopy of the deckhouse and rolled up the flaps to let in air. They lay there dazed with heat.

Michael worried at first about the Land Cruiser, but after a few hours he would almost have welcomed its arrival. Perhaps Kirsty was right. Perhaps they were going to die. All because he had believed in a secret dream. Was it wrong to believe in a dream?

He remembered the prospector's remark about other people's dreams and he thought of the prospector's dream. The prospector seemed to know that he doubted his story.

Perhaps it was true that he didn't have room

for anyone else's dreams — or for anyone else in his dreams.

Anyone.

They came silently on carefully placed, padded feet, in a long-necked swaying gait — archly amused-looking creatures, three tied together; and on the first rode an old woman in a bush hat, with long hair beneath it that fell around her shoulders like a grey tent.

She made a whooshing sound to the camel she rode and, with long-limbed grace, the creature collapsed to the sand in stages, first with one knee lowered to the ground, then the other, then the hind legs before the forelimbs were settled, and it settled its entire weight on its breast pad.

The old woman dismounted. 'It's a mirage inside a mirage,' she said, shaking her head in amazement at the sight of the Sail-Railer. Michael and Kirsty blinked in surprise at the new arrival. They slid out of the shade of the Sail-Railer and stepped onto the fiery ground to meet her.

'Hello, ducks.'

'Hi, we're stuck here,' Kirsty said.

'What are you doing here?'

'Sweating,' the prospector called from the deckhouse.

'Do you have any water?

'A bit, but we need more.'

'There's water up ahead,' she said. 'Alice can smell it. Camels can always smell water, you know.'

'Could your camels tow us there?' Michael asked.

The idea seemed to amuse her. 'I suppose we could. I'll get a rope.' She went to the crouched camel and opened a saddlebag, taking out a long length of rope. She tied one end to the saddle and ran it back to the Sail-Railer, where Michael took it eagerly and secured it to the front.

'You'd better remove that sail,' the camel lady said. 'Alice goes slowly enough as it is — a sedate twelve kilometres an hour is about her best speed, but she can keep it up for days.'

Michael furled the sail.

'There's an old siding up ahead with a water pump. I'll have to ride there on Alice or she won't go. We'll have a chat when we get there.'

She mounted the camel again and at another whooshing sound from her it rose, thrusting its head forward with a jerk, hauling itself to its knees with an hydraulic-sounding hiss, then lifting its hindquarters. Next it lifted one foreleg, planting it flat on the sand, then jacked its 500 kilograms of weight into a full-standing position.

The old woman went swiftly up as if ascending in a fireman's crane. She looked very dignified up there, Michael thought. She gave them a salute, turned the camel and set off along the side of the railway line, the other two camels following, stepping wide of the tracks.

They were moving again! They rolled through the quivering waves of heat, towed by the old woman and her camels. The creatures looked uneasy about the trundling Sail-Railer.

'I don't believe it,' Kirsty said. 'What's an old lady doing out here?'

'She might ask the same of you,' the prospector said. 'What are you doing out here?'

'We're off our trolley,' Kirsty joked, cheering.

'Maybe she's off her trolley, too,' Michael said.

'Something's strange about her,' Kirsty said, agreeing. 'Did you notice? She seemed surprised to see us, but she wasn't surprised about the railway line. She knew it was here. She also knows there's a siding up ahead with a water pump.'

'She's probably half-mad from the heat and the loneliness,' Michael said. 'I suppose it does that to people.'

The prospector did not miss the suggestion behind his remark.

'You think that's what's happened to me, do you? Well, you're wrong; I'm not half-mad. I am *totally* mad — or at least I was once. But I'm trying to make up for it.'

8
Tracking the past

IT WAS LIKE AN OASIS at the siding. Palms grew near a rusting water tank that stood on long, skeletal iron legs. The old woman took them to a bore pump and opened it to allow water to gush out. Michael, Kirsty and the prospector plunged their heads under the spouting jet.

Michael gasped as the cool water rivered down the inside of his shirt. He made a tunnel of his mouth and took a roaring express train of water into his throat, gulping it joyously down. The old woman looked on benignly, like a grandmother watching small grandchildren playing in the bath. Michael took the opportunity to refill their water bottle.

Afterwards they sat on a pile of old sleepers in the shade of the tank to dry. The wind came up again, speeding evaporation and cooling them more. The camel woman squatted cross-legged on the ground in front of them as if drawing near to a campfire to warm herself. The sight of children seemed to delight her. She wore glasses and her eyes darted like little birds above them.

'Enjoy the water, ducks?'

'Yes, and I know how a duck feels,' Kirsty said. 'That was fantastic.'

'Are you their father?' she shot at the prospector, who sat further back in the shadow of the tank.

'Not me. I'm just a passenger they picked up along the way.'

'Have we met before? I seem to remember your face.'

'I don't think that's possible.'

'Suppose you tell me what you're doing here.'

'Ask young Michael — he's the captain of our ship.'

'Well, Michael. How did you get here?'

He shrugged. 'The wind blew us here. I don't know how it happened.'

'The wind blew you here!' She laughed heartily. 'That's one thing I miss most about children. Their *imaginations*. Anything is possible at your age, isn't it! Well, don't let me be the one who says it isn't so.' She gave a wink. 'I'll accept your explanation.'

Kirsty was just as curious about her. 'What are *you* doing here?'

'Following the train tracks.'

'Then the tracks do exist?'

'They do if you have eyes to see. I'm a very good tracker, you see. I'm tracking the past — the route the old Ghan took between Adelaide and Alice Springs. I'm going into the red heart.'

Tracks.

Did she mean tracks as in railway tracks — or tracks as in marks left behind after they'd ripped up the line? Michael was about to ask her, when she spoke again.

'I'm a bit of a bush poet as well as an historian. I've written a poem about the old Ghan train. Would you like to hear it? It's called "Ghost Tracks".' Her eyes rolled up above her glasses and her eyes fluttered above them as if she were reading words written in the air:

Where rail tracks meet on the red horizon,
I'll find the old Ghan train.
Between the lines of infinity,
I'll see her run again.

Her whistle shriek, her clanking rush,
The hiss of an iron sigh;
She'll ride again on her long lost tracks,
Just as in days gone by.

Her smoke once joined the horizon's span,
As she scribbled across the chart,
Writing the legend of the Ghan,
Across territory of the heart.

Where rail tracks meet on the red horizon,
I'll find the old Ghan train.
Where rail tracks meet on the red horizon,
I'll see her ride again.

Kirsty applauded. 'That's beautiful.'

'Thankyou, ducks.'

Michael had to agree. The camel lady had written about the old Ghan train just as he liked to think about her.

The old Ghan train.

Perhaps you could share a dream. Perhaps he should make a bit more space for others who dreamed. Like this curious camel lady following the lost train tracks. And the prospector, following a map with a cross on it. He looked at the man in the shadows of the overhead tank. Maybe it was true. Maybe they really would discover a reef of gold if they sailed to the end of the line.

The camel lady followed his line of vision. She addressed the prospector again. 'What did you think of the poem?' she asked. He had been silent.

'It saddened me,' he said. 'I nearly went on the old Ghan train a very long time ago. I wish I had. It might have changed things.'

'Don't I know you, sir? I've seen your face.'

'We've never met.'

'The furnace of the interior is full of sadness,' she agreed. 'Many partings, many dyings. Prospectors, adventurers, explorers: their faces fill our history books and their loss is part of Australia's empty terror. You can feel a great missing and a longing out there. Even here in this very spot. I feel it strongly now.'

'We've delayed enough,' the prospector said abruptly. 'We've got a journey to finish.'

Michael thought it was his place as captain of the Sail-Railer to decide when to move on, but he agreed with the prospector. Kirsty looked uncertain. She turned to Michael. 'Do you want to go on, Michael?'

'You don't have to go on,' the camel lady said, taking them both in with a look of entreaty. 'It's been quite an adventure already, hasn't it? Come back with me. I've got two empty camels to take you home.'

The oasis had refreshed Michael. 'We'll go on,' he said.

'Are you sure, ducks? Dreams can be selfish things and you should never follow them at the expense of others. Nor should you follow them lightly. It's one thing to follow your dream — it's another to just blow along with it. This country can kill you if you aren't careful. Without water and shade, you can die in just nine hours. There are many stories of people who have broken down in their cars and foolishly left them to go walking off into the desert in search of help.'

'How do you survive out here?' Kirsty said.

'I'm an old bushie and I know how to survive. I've done my research and I know where the water holes are located and, if I forget, Alice here will remind me — she can nose them out, half-a-day away. People can survive if they know how.

'I met a man and his wife a few weeks back, parked off the side of the road. No help had come for days and they had run out of water. Wisely, they stayed with their vehicle. They knew how to get water by making dew traps. They dug holes and covered them with plastic from shopping bags they cut open, spreading them over the depression with stones on top to collect more dew and hold the plastic down. A lot of dew falls in the desert. They made themselves enough water to stay alive until help came.'

'We'll be all right,' Michael said.

'I hope you're right. There are some strange people on the track.' She looked at the prospector. 'Were you out there prospecting on your own?' she said. 'Before these two young people kindly gave you a lift, I mean. You didn't happen to have a companion at any stage?'

'I'm a loner,' the prospector said. 'I've always worked alone.'

'Hmm. I met a couple of policemen who said there were a pair of bad men on the loose. They attacked a lone prospector and stole his gold. They asked me to keep an eye open — law of the track, you know.'

'I'm alone. Always alone.'

'Until now.'

He still looked alone, Michael thought, even now. He was trying to stay alone, keeping apart from the group. A shadow of uneasiness like a passing bird flitted over Michael's mind.

'Well, just be careful, ducks, all of you.'

They said goodbye to the camel lady and thanked her again, and they had a last, long drink from the bore.

'That's right, store it up like a camel.'

They returned to the Sail-Railer. She waved them goodbye as if seeing them off on holiday at a train station, waving a red handkerchief. She looked forlorn to see them go.

Michael wasn't sure what started the doubt.

Perhaps it was the warning about the bad men on the loose and the prospector's eagerness to get away, but also his shyness about answering the camel lady's questions.

'I met a couple of policemen who said there were a pair of bad men on the loose. . .' A couple of policemen. He remembered the whip aerial on the Land Cruiser. It had a radio. Was it a police radio? Were the two pursuers policemen?

If they were. . . who was the prospector?

9
Crisis of doubt

NOW IT WAS MICHAEL'S TURN to examine the prospector as if he were a rock sample of dubious value. The man was dozing in the deckhouse, his hat over his face. What did he know about him? What would a sample analysis of the facts show?

He began by looking at the surface evidence. They'd found him wandering alone, with an injured leg. No prospecting equipment, no compass, no water or provisions. His mysterious appearance should have set alarm bells ringing.

Then there was the hint of more below the surface, the promise of discovery. The map. The talk of treasure.

After surface examination, Michael found himself crushing the evidence between the surfaces of hard doubts. If the man really was a lost and injured prospector, why hadn't he let them take him back to the cattle station? He seemed eager to avoid people, including the camel lady. This talk of gold was just a trick to lure them on — to what? Michael ran these ideas through a clear stream of thought and he did not come up with gold, but with grey and muddy fears. The man was a risk to them. They had to get rid of him. Throw him off the Sail-Railer, if necessary.

'What are you plotting?' Kirsty said, her eyes watching him from under the cool brim of her straw hat. He put a finger to his lips and pointed to the front of the Sail-Railer. He went ahead and, mystified, she followed.

'What is it Michael? You look as if you've seen a ghost.'

'Worse than that. Sit down, Kirsty. We have to talk.'

They sat beside each other at the front of the Sail-Railer, their legs dangling over the front, the sleepers flicking underneath them as they travelled.

'Well?'

'It's him. I'm throwing him off.'

'You're doing no such thing. Why?'

'I don't think he's a prospector. I don't believe a word he's telling us, and worse — I reckon those two men chasing him are policemen. I think we've got a criminal on board.'

He shared his suspicions with Kirsty in detail and reminded her of what the camel lady had said. He expected fear from her. He expected panic. Even admiration for his deductive powers.

But it was always hard to guess how Kirsty would react. It was like the time when he first revealed the Sail-Railer to her and she walked over to it and gave it a kick with the toe of her sneaker. She was no more impressed with this latest revelation.

'So you just want to throw him overboard and forget about him?' Her wise, sisterly eyes seemed to expect a lot better of Michael.

'Don't make it sound so bad, Kirsty. This isn't the ocean. He isn't going to drown, you know.'

'No, he won't drown, but water will kill him just the same, or at least the lack of it will.'

'That's not the issue. The issue is him or us. He could be a killer.'

'If you threw him off — you *would* be a killer.'

'He's got to go.'

'I don't agree.'

'The Sail-Railer's mine. I'm the captain.

This is my ship.'

'Well, this is mutiny,' she said. 'Because I say absolutely no.'

'Then I'll throw him off. I can do it.'

'Maybe you'd like to throw me off, too, because I don't fit into your plans.'

'Don't be a goof.'

'You throw him off and I'll go with him.'

'You'd do that for a criminal?'

'We don't know he's a criminal, but we do know he's a human being. I don't believe he's a criminal. I trust him. You've got to have a bit of faith in people; you've got to trust your likings and not just your suspicions.'

'Great,' Michael said. 'He's won you over. Maybe I should let the two of you go on without me.'

'Grow up, Michael.'

'That's it. I'm going to face him.' Michael stood up.

'You mean you're going to accuse him.'

'Same thing. Who cares?' Michael felt in his pocket for the sheath knife. He crawled under the sail to the prospector, whose legs were sticking out as far as the mast. He rose to stand over him and gave the man's good leg a kick.

The prospector shot up and banged his head on the deckhouse roof. 'What's the matter?'

'You,' Michael said.

Kirsty came behind Michael and grabbed his arm to tug him back. 'Put that away.'

'Leave me, Kirsty. I'm trying to save us both.'

'Let me guess,' the prospector said, eyeing the boy's hand. 'You want a turn in the shade of the deckhouse?'

'I want some real answers.'

'Ah,' the prospector said, as if understanding dawned on him. 'So it's time to give account, is it?'

'Yes. You can begin by telling us the truth about those people chasing us. They wouldn't happen to be policemen?'

'I hope not. It would be a sad day for the Territory if they were. They're the bad men who attacked a prospector and stole his gold. I know. You see, I was the prospector.'

The prospector smiled pleasantly. Michael looked at Kirsty as if she could confirm the story. She wouldn't look at him. Michael felt as if he had stepped into an unseen hole. He felt a hot flush of embarrassment rise to his face, but he had gone too far and the momentum of his aggression carried him on. 'Then how come you don't have any prospector's equipment?' he said suspiciously.

'I escaped from them, leaving everything behind. . . does that make any sense?' Maddeningly, it did.

The sounds of the Sail-Railer receded in Michael's ears. He had a sudden desire to jump overboard himself. 'Well, don't try any funny stuff with us, that's all,' he said lamely. He put the sheath knife back in his pocket.

'You mean like kicking people while they're asleep and waving sheath knives in their faces? Who'd do a thing like that?'

Kirsty turned in disgust and went back to the front of the Sail-Railer. Michael wished the Sail-Railer were six times the size.

There was nowhere to go and hide from his shame. The prospector smiled at him. 'I understand your feelings,' he said.

Michael flinched. He couldn't go on looking at the man. Mercifully, the prospector pulled the brim of his hat over his face and lay back to doze.

Michael did not dare go to Kirsty. He squatted on the deck beside the sail and sat gazing sightlessly at the passing countryside. He knew what she'd say to him if he went to her. 'Go back and apologise to him.'

He flamed against the idea. He wouldn't do it. She couldn't push him around. She'd been pushing him around ever since he'd shown her the Sail-Railer. She couldn't play mother with him.

Her words came back like twinges of discomfort: 'You've got to have a bit of faith in people; you've got to trust your likings and not just your suspicions.'

'I'm sorry,' he said to the prospector.

'I forgive you,' the prospector said, his voice muffled through the brim of his bush hat. 'But there's a young lady sitting at the front who hasn't quite done that yet. Don't disappoint her, son. She's a special sort of person.'

He gulped and went under the sail. Kirsty sat with her back to him. She heard him coming, but didn't turn her head.

'I'm hopeless, aren't I?' he said.

She turned. 'Did you apologise to him?'

'Yes.'

'Then you're not hopeless.'

'I am; I'm hopeless.'

Her face softened. 'Not to me, you're not. You see, I have faith in you, too. Your head's a bit too full of dreams right now, but it won't always be and one day there'll be room for others.'

He felt very small and humbled. 'I hope I didn't scare him too badly,' he said.

'I don't think so.'

'Why?'

She smiled. 'That knife you were waving around. You still had the leather sheath on it.'

'You're kidding?'

'It's true.'

He laughed. She laughed, too. He laughed again.

His laughter was a bit wild and cracked-sounding. He had gone right to the edge of a giddying drop and stepped back again and relief poured through him.

A wedge-tailed eagle, a bird with one of the largest wingspans on earth, sailed in harmony with the wind above them, its wingtip feathers playing the thermals like invisible keys.

'Are we getting close?' Michael said to the prospector. 'You never look at your map.'

'I don't have to. It's impressed on my brain.'

'Then why do you carry it?'

'It's a touchstone. A link with the past. And the answer is yes, we are very close now.'

'Where is the spot?'

'A few kilometres before an abandoned settlement, in a valley, where the track runs past a hillside shaped like the head of a dingo. It's a short walk from there.'

'May I see the map?'

'You're the captain.' The prospector took out the map and gave it to Michael, taking care that it did not blow away in the wind. Michael flattened it on the deck and Kirsty craned over his shoulder to look. He found the curve in the track and a spot marked 'Dingo's Head'. He saw the cross and a dotted line leading from the track to meet it.

He touched the cross with his finger and shivered. Kirsty noticed. 'You've come out in goose bumps. What is it?'

'Tell me about your treasure,' he said to the prospector. 'Is it a vein of gold? How wide is it? How deep do you think?'

'About one metre wide and two metres deep.'

Two metres deep. Michael saw it in his mind, a flash of gold lightning running through the red earth. No, it wouldn't be red earth. If it were gold reef country, there would be quartz or ironstone lying about.

'X marks the spot,' he said under his breath.

'No Xs, please,' the prospector said. 'Xs are what is wrong with the world. X is for things we are embarrassed to say. What you see on the map is not an X. It's a cross.'

'A cross, an X — what does it matter? They

both mean the same thing. They both mark a spot.'

'A cross means a bit more,' the prospector said.

Kirsty nodded wisely as if she agreed with him, but it seemed a fine point to Michael. He rolled up the map and gave it back to the man. They climbed a rise and edged over the crest before running down into a plain.

The red Land Cruiser was waiting in the middle of the plain, facing them, its wheels straddling the track, its bull-bars aggressively set for impact.

10
Boarding party

MICHAEL MADE A GRAB FOR the ropes that tied down the sail, and hoisted up the spar, collapsing the sail. It slowed them but, even with the sail gone, the Sail-Railer sped on, drawing momentum from the grade.

'We'd better jump,' Michael said.

'I can't,' the prospector said.

'We'd better run and hide.'

'Hide?'

They were in the middle of flat saltbush country. Only a rabbit could hide out here.

They were closing with the red Land Cruiser, but it was further away than it had first seemed and not in the lowest part of the plain, but at the beginning of a slight rise. The pursuers wanted to stop the Sail-Railer, but they didn't want to destroy their vehicle in doing it.

'The trolley could tip over when we hit,' Michael warned them. 'It's safer to jump.'

'You two jump,' the prospector said. He flattened himself on the deck, bracing himself with a foot on the mast and grabbing the support posts of the deckhouse roof. 'There's only room for one of us to hang on properly.'

'But they'll catch you.'

'Can't be helped.'

'We'd better do it, Kirsty. If this thing rolls, the iron wheels could squash us. I'll tell you when to jump.'

The two men had climbed out of the Land Cruiser and were standing on either side of the track, ready to grab them when they stopped. They were worried about the speed of the Sail-Railer, Michael thought, noticing their uneasy expressions. They were already wincing as if preparing for the bang of the collision.

One of the men shouted an instruction to the other and pointed to the Land Cruiser. The second man ran back to the Land Cruiser. He jumped into the driver's seat, started up the engine and slammed the gears into reverse, backing the vehicle along the track, evidently hoping to ride with the blow of the Sail-Railer and lessen the impact.

The man near the track jumped aside. The

Sail-Railer flicked past. It was only metres away from the Land Cruiser, the vehicle's bull-bars blocking the way like an iron gate. Michael saw alarm widen the eyes of the driver.

'Jump!' he shouted to Kirsty. 'Fall and roll in the direction of travel and keep your knees bent.'

Kirsty put out her hand and he took it.

'Now!' They jumped.

The Sail-Railer hit the steel bull-bars with a hollow bang like empty freight cars slammed together in a shunting yard and the Land Cruiser shot back along the tracks under the impact. The Sail-Railer reared on the rails with the prospector still clinging to the deck. It fell heavily back, landing squarely onto the rails with a loud *clang*.

The man at the trackside ignored Michael and Kirsty and ran to the Sail-Railer. The one in the Land Cruiser cut the engine and jumped out of the cab to join his companion who was at the Sail-Railer, looking down at the prospector.

The prospector sat up and gave them a numb stare. They dragged him off the trolley to the side of the track.

'Leave him alone!' Michael shouted from a safe distance.

They ignored him. They searched the

prospector who put up no struggle. One of them turned up the map from the prospector's pocket.

'Let's get him into the car,' he said. The prospector threw an apologetic glance at Michael and Kirsty and shrugged. The two men bundled him into the Land Cruiser. Then, as an afterthought, one of the men came back along the line, carrying a knife in his hand. He turned a hard look in their direction.

'Let's run,' Kirsty said.

'He'll never catch us,' Michael said, not moving.

'Relax,' the man said. 'I'm not going to touch you, but in case you kids get any ideas about following, I'm going to take the wind out of your sails.' He jumped aboard the Sail-Railer, the knife blade flashing in his hand. To their puzzlement, he released the sail.

'Oh, no,' Michael said, as the man's intention became clear. Michael started forward, but Kirsty held his arm.

The man slashed the ground sheet, slicing a large X in the orange plastic. The wind poured through the gap, turning the sail into quadrants that flapped like pennants.

'Perhaps we should have gone with the camel lady,' Kirsty said forlornly. The man gave them a cheery wave. He returned to the Land Cruiser. The vehicle drove away, travelling parallel with the line.

They weren't policemen, Michael thought. Policemen wouldn't leave two kids stranded in the outback.

As if to taunt them, the wind now rose in strength as Michael and Kirsty walked back to the track through the saltbush scrub to rejoin the Sail-Railer. They had both lost their hats in the fall from the trolley. They picked them up. The wind blew Kirsty's hat off again. She went after it. It added to their mood of frustration.

A freshening wind was a fat lot of good to them now, Michael thought bitterly. Without a sail, the wind was no more use to them than the sun that beat down on the plain. He had doubted the prospector's story once and now he burnt with shame and remorse.

Kirsty held her straw hat on her head with one hand. 'Maybe we should leave the trolley and start walking,' she said in a small, helpless voice.

'In which direction?'

'Back, I suppose.'

'We're better off staying with the trolley until

dark. At least we have the shade of the deckhouse for shelter.'

Michael looked at the giant, fluttering X slashed into their sail. 'X marks the spot,' he said ironically, 'and a spot is exactly what we're in now.'

An X marked the spot on the prospector's map and now it marked the spot where the prospector's dream had ended. The pursuers would no doubt steal his claim and make certain he was never seen again.

'I agree with the prospector. I don't like Xs,' Kirsty said. 'I think it's a cross. Do you remember what the prospector said? A cross means a bit more.'

As he looked at it, thinking of it as a cross and not an X, he wondered what extra meaning a cross could have. A few ideas occurred to him. An X meant error, cancellation, wrong. But a cross meant hope, putting things right. There was a lot that needed putting right, Michael thought. His judgment of the prospector was one. The hole in the sail was another.

'It's time to do some repairing,' he said.

He separated some strands of rope to make lengths of thread and Kirsty came up with a perfect needle — a metal hairpin which she had used to secure her hat to her hair. Michael used the loop of the hairpin as an eyelet, threading a strand of rope through it, and he pulled the two protective knobs off the ends of the hairpin and rubbed the two arms against the railway line to form a single, sharp point. He took the sail down and sat with it on the ground. He held two sides of the slashed surface together and made a stab at one side with the hairpin needle. He speared his finger on the other side, and let out a yelp.

'I can see you never went to sewing classes,' Kirsty said, amused. 'Let me have a go.' She took over. Ignoring the late afternoon heat, she squatted on the ground to sew. Engrossed in her work, her tongue peeked from the corner of her mouth. The needle went through the plastic easily and she drew the threads tight. It took time. Michael gave her a drink from the water bottle during a break, and they each had another shortbread biscuit.

When she had put the last stitch into the sail, she said: 'There, the cross has made this stronger. If it tears again, it will tear somewhere else, not on this cross. The weakest part is now the strongest.'

He caught an extra meaning in what she said. Her words impressed him as much as her sewing. It reminded him of the time when she asked for the wind to blow. There was a calm assurance in the way she spoke. It filled him with certainty that what she said was true. The weakest part was now the strongest.

Michael rigged up the sail anew and sheeted it to the deck. He didn't even have to give the Sail-Railer a push. The repaired sail drew in a big breath of air and filled out, stretching tightly as a drum. The trolley rolled forward.

The stitched cross on the sail stood out bravely and seemed to taunt the wind.

The Sail-Railer had never run so swiftly. Her iron wheels sang a bright song, no longer rusty from too little use.

'It's a safe bet they'll be following the railway line,' Michael said. 'It's also a safe bet that if it gets dark before they get to the site, they'll camp for the night. With any luck, we'll catch them.'

'What are we going to do if we catch them?'

'We'll think of something,' he said.

'We? That's your department,' Kirsty laughed. 'I did the sewing.'

The wind blew animals onto the scene. They saw kangaroos bound gracefully by as if suspended on strings, and a solitary emu stared aloofly at their passing. Rabbits popped up to look at them and, in a blink, were gone again, scattering as abruptly as they appeared.

They thought they saw the camel lady far away, but it was only a herd of feral camels strung out across the skyline.

They sailed through late afternoon and dusk into night.

There was still no sign of the Land Cruiser.

The stars, like diamonds forged in the searing temperatures of day, came out to blaze down on them and the moon lit the dun-coloured bluebush in a ghostly glow.

'Do you think the old Ghan train still runs on these lines?' Michael said.

'Yes,' Kirsty nodded, 'but only in the minds of people like the camel lady and the prospector.'

'And me.'

'You believe it?'

'Maybe. What would you do if you saw a bright light up ahead and it wasn't the Land Cruiser, but the old Ghan steaming towards us?'

'Jump, but I don't fancy doing it in the dark.'

A piercing shriek like a steam whistle hit their startled ears. 'What was that?' asked Kirsty.

Michael saw a large bird — perhaps an owl — dive and arc away into the darkness. 'Just a night bird. Don't be scared,' he said, partly to calm himself. His own heart fluttered like a bird's.

'Thanks for making me jumpy. Can we forget about ghost trains, please?'

'Sorry,' he said, 'just dreaming out loud.' He surprised himself. He was starting to share his dreams.

In the clear dry air he saw their camp fire from several kilometres away. They were camped between a cluster of hillocks for protection from the wind. Michael raised the sail a quarter of the way up the mast, breaking the Sail-Railer's speed, allowing her to coast the rest of the distance to the edge of the camp site.

They crept closer. They saw the two men seated at a camp fire. Michael took the sail up further, though still leaving a small area of sail exposed to the breeze.

'Here's my plan,' Michael said. 'You stay on the Sail-Railer and coast quietly past the camp fire. When you get a hundred metres beyond it, take the sail up all the way and stop. I'm going to try to rescue the prospector. If I'm lucky, we'll meet you on the other side. Get ready to cram on sail. There could be a chase.'

'You're not leaving me here,' she said. 'The days when girls sit around while boys do all the exciting bits are over.'

'All right,' he said. 'You go and tackle the guy who's armed with the knife and I'll stay here.'

'Don't be too long,' she said, changing her mind quickly. 'I don't want to be left alone in the bush in the dark.'

Michael jumped off the Sail-Railer, landing firmly on the trackside. The wind was turbulent. It seemed to be shifting direction, making the patch of sail on the Sail-Railer rattle against the mast, but the Sail-Railer kept moving. Perhaps the cluster of hillocks was chanelling the wind in strange directions. The wind was a help, though. It howled over the bluebush, making it unlikely that the men would hear them. Michael pocketed the sheath knife.

'I'll try to be quick,' he said.

He left Kirsty and the Sail-Railer edging slowly along the rails and, keeping low, he picked his way over the bluebush to the camp site. When he drew close enough to hear the men's voices, he went lower, crawling in a circle to come up behind the parked Land Cruiser. There was no sign of the prospector. He must be tied up inside, Michael guessed.

The two men were drinking coffee from enamel mugs and discussing the map which one of them held. Michael could smell the roasted aroma of the coffee. It reminded him of his thirst. He tried to swallow, but his tongue stuck drily in his throat. He was near the Land Cruiser now. He went to the far side door. Cautiously raising himself, he peered into the cabin.

The prospector lay in the back seat of the Land Cruiser. Found you. Michael tried the door gently. Locked.

He noticed that the window was open a fraction to stop the car's windows from misting up. There was enough room to slide his arm inside. Carefully, he slid his arm through the gap and pulled the door safety catch.

He didn't expect a car alarm to go off in the middle of the outback. He couldn't have been more startled if a floodlight had been snapped on him.

11
Fighting back

KEEP GOING, MICHAEL THOUGHT, with the alarm howling in his ears.

He threw open the door and swept the sheath knife out of his pocket. He slid the blade between the prospector's ankles, sawed at the ropes and freed his legs and then went for the rope between the man's wrists.

He got further than he could have hoped. His knife blade went through the last strand of rope as a strong pair of hands grabbed him from behind and dragged him away.

The prospector, thinking quickly, made no move to run, but lay with his arms and legs pressed together as if still firmly bound.

The attacker spun Michael around. It was the man with the map. He still had it protruding from his shirt pocket.

'It's that kid. How did you get here so fast?' The other man came over. The firelight lit the despair in Michael's face.

'Good thing I set the car alarm. You just can't get away from crime and break-ins — even out here in the outback,' he said.

'What are you doing here, son? Still looking for trouble? Do I have to cut up more than your sail?' he said, the knife appearing in his hand. 'Where is that contraption on rails?'

Michael wished at that moment that he didn't know the answer to the man's question, but appallingly he did.

The wind had changed direction. The Sail-Railer came trundling backwards in line with the camp fire. He could see the standing figure of Kirsty struggling with the sail, passing like a piece of moving stage scenery.

'It's right behind you,' Michael said. The man half-turned. He caught sight of Kirsty on the Sail-Railer. Michael snatched the map from the man's top pocket. At the same moment, the prospector kicked out, knocking the man back into the bushes. Michael head-butted the second man who grunted in surprise and, while he was bent double, the prospector jumped out to shove him into the bush.

Michael and the prospector ran. Michael

held onto the prospector's arm to take some of the weight off his leg. They ran like a pair of contestants in a three-legged race.

The wind had grown even wilder and more buffeting. It changed direction crazily as they ran for the line. Kirsty came trundling forward, still comically struggling with the sail.

'Great sailing,' Michael said, pushing the prospector on board and jumping on after him. Michael sheeted the sail securely. The Sail-Railer quickened her pace. She took off along the rails.

'What made you do that — come for me?' the prospector said in wonder.

'You've got a ticket to ride to the end of the line and that's where we're taking you,' he said, giving the man back his map.

'You're quite a find,' the prospector said.

The Land Cruiser's two bright eyes made holes of light in the dark. They heard the growl of its engine, even above the sound of the wind and the iron song of the Sail-Railer's wheels. It was coming up behind them, racing along the edge of the railway line. The headlights hit the orange sail and lit it like sunset. The cross stood out vividly like a scar.

'We can't outrun them,' the prospector said.

'They're going to overtake us and block the line.'

If only they had more sail — or a spinnaker. The blanket. It was worth a try.

Kirsty and the prospector held one end of a blanket and Michael the other, filling the gap underneath the sail. The blanket bellied in the wind. The force of it tugged their arms, but the Sail-Railer gave an extra surge.

The Land Cruiser hit a dip and slowed. The Sail-Railer pulled away again, widening the gap between them. The Land Cruiser put on more speed.

'What do we do?' Kirsty said. 'They'll do a lot worse than cut our sail this time.'

'If they catch us,' Michael said defiantly. They hit a down grade and picked up speed.

Kirsty lost her grip on the blanket and it snapped out of her hand, also tearing out of the prospector's hand, but Michael held onto his end. It trailed uselessly ahead of him like a giant woollen scarf.

The Land Cruiser lay fifty metres behind them. Its headlights, on high beam, lit the deck and the tracks like a stage and threw their shadows on the sand.

They hit a small rise and cruised over it. Michael peered ahead along the rails. The following Land Cruiser hit another hump. For a second its lights spilled over their heads, then dipped briefly as it came over the hump, but it was long enough to reveal a form up ahead — the pale uprights of a bridge.

Hope surged in Michael. If only they could reach it before the Land Cruiser overtook them.

He needed to slow them. How? What did he have on board? Canvas bag, water bottle, the prospector's gnarled walking stick...

Had the Land Cruiser seen the bridge? It seemed to be coming up faster. It was almost at their tail.

The blanket. Perhaps he could throw it onto the windscreen and block their view. It fluttered in his hands.

No good. It wouldn't work. Once the blanket left his hands, it would slip away like a cloud. It wouldn't stick — unless it was wet.

The water. Did he dare waste their precious water?

'Give me the water bottle,' he said to Kirsty. 'And the other blanket.' She dived into the deckhouse for the bottle. The prospector found the other blanket.

Michael made a nest of the blanket in his arms, ripped the cap off the water bottle and slopped water into the centre. The blanket gathered weight as if a cold animal had crawled inside it. 'Squash it in,' he told Kirsty. She understood and helped him squeeze the blanket, spreading moisture through the fibres. Michael felt cold water trickle through his fingers and run down his legs.

The Land Cruiser was set to overtake them. It started to move out. Michael tossed the water bottle into the prospector's hands. Then, holding the sodden ball of wet blanket in both hands, he took aim at the windscreen and threw it like a basketball. It hit the windscreen and stuck like a wet sack, but it had missed the driver's side, landing instead on the passenger's side. The driver swerved, but came back on course.

The prospector and Kirsty were already slopping water into the second blanket. Kirsty did not wait for Michael, but took aim with the second blanket.

Michael stiffened. He hoped her aim was better than her sailing. She let fly. The wet blanket landed squarely in front of the driver, pasted over the windscreen as neatly as a car cover, obscuring his view.

The Sail-Railer went onto the bridge, the sound of its wheels turning hollow as it rolled out over an inky void. The Land Cruiser, blind now, did not see the approaching bridge, nor the drop.

It sailed over the gap.

'Good shot, Kirsty.'

'I'm in the netball team at school,' Kirsty said, by way of explanation.

'Good girl,' the prospector said.

12

A cross marks the spot

THEY TRAVELLED ON THROUGH THE NIGHT. They were without water now and thirsty after their struggle — but at least they were free of their pursuers, Michael thought. They had also rescued the prospector and that made Michael feel that he had begun to put things right.

Michael took up their sail a bit so that they kept to a moderate speed and he lay down on the deck to rest. The three of them lay with their heads and bodies inside the deckhouse and their legs sticking out across the deck. Without blankets, they had only their shared body heat to keep them warm.

Half-an-hour after sun-up, they sighted Dingo's

Head, a hill with a sharp, snout-like projection and two triangles of rock like erect ears.

'We're near the end of our journey,' the prospector said. 'We can walk from here.' Michael took up their sail and the Sail-Railer slowed, squeaking, to a halt.

The prospector took the map out of his pocket and opened it, thoughtfully touching a spot with his finger, even though he claimed the details were etched in his mind. It was as if he were touching a lucky charm, Michael thought. The prospector swallowed. When he looked up his eyes shone, but it was not the greedy sheen of a man dreaming of gold. It was a light of tenderness.

The prospector grabbed his stick. 'This way,' he said. They walked. The prospector went ahead, moving eagerly on the stick. He winced occasionally, but was driven by the nearness of his goal.

Michael examined the terrain as they walked. The ground was hard and red with clumps of bluebush spreading in every direction. The place puzzled him. There was no sign of quartz or ironstone.

Was this the right place? Had the map — or the prospector's memory — failed him?

They kept walking. A doubt began to

shadow Michael's footsteps. This wasn't gold reef country. He had read too many books about it to be mistaken.

The prospector was breathing deeply. They had come upon a clearing where a small, burnt-out stone cottage stood in blackened despair. 'There,' he said in a shaky whisper like a sigh. He stopped.

'Is this the place?' Michael said. 'Is this the cross on your map?'

'Over there.'

The prospector wasn't looking at the burnt-out cottage. He had directed his gleaming eyes to a small mound that supported a lonely stone cross. Beside it lay a smaller mound with a second, smaller cross. The prospector flung his stick away and hobbled to the mounds, giving a cry and falling onto his knees.

It was a grave site.

'This. . . was my treasure,' he said. 'I left them to follow a stupid, selfish dream of my own. They died while I was away — my wife and baby son. They had been working their way up north, but perished in a fire in this cottage, in the home of a farmer who gave them shelter. A stranger gave me this map, years later. I have been trying to come back to this spot ever since. . .'

'You mean it was a gravestone,' Michael said. 'The cross on your map. . .'

'Yes, this is my cross,' he said, turning obsessed eyes at Michael, 'and I've carried it for a long, long time. I left my real treasure to go off in search of . . . fool's treasure. Like you, Michael, I didn't have much room for anyone else in my dreams. Anyone.'

'We're awfully sorry,' Kirsty said. She had tears in her eyes.

'Thankyou, Kirsty. A person like you who knows how to share dreams also knows how to share sorrows. But I must ask you and Michael to leave me alone. I have things to think and feelings to feel alone in this place.'

Kirsty tugged on Michael's shirtsleeve and led him away, taking him towards the burnt out cottage.

'I don't want to go inside,' Michael said. 'Let's sit out here.' They sat on stones in the shade of an ironbark.

'This was his dream,' Michael said. 'To visit a grave. It's not a gold reef at all.'

'He never said it was gold.'

'He said it was two metres deep and about one metre wide.'

'And so it was. That's the shape of a grave.'

'But he let us think the cross was a treasure.

It was the wrong impression.'

'Not wrong, Michael. An X is wrong. This was a cross.'

They didn't see the willy-willy come up. It swept out of the bush, ripping up leaves and dust in its spiral claws. Kirsty called a warning to the kneeling prospector.

He turned to give an understanding nod of his head, but he did not rise. The willy-willy ran towards him, growing more dense and swollen with debris. Then it covered him and he was lost from sight.

The willy-willy moved on.

The prospector had gone from their sight as if snatched up by the wind. They looked for him and called out his name, but he had vanished.

Michael felt stripped of something, like the bare ground over which the willy-willy had passed. But it wasn't a feeling of disappointment. It was a clean feeling as if something had gone from himself that needed to go.

'He's gone with the willy-willy,' Michael said.

'But he couldn't have.'

'That's how he came, remember.' A willy-willy had brought him into their lives and now one had taken him away.

They were tired and thirsty. There had been

a settlement here once. Was there a bore nearby? They looked but could not find one. Perhaps it had dried up years ago. They went back through the bush to the Sail-Railer.

'Like you, Michael, I didn't have much room for anyone else in my dreams. Anyone.'

The words spun around in Michael's mind like the willy-willy. The prospector's real treasure wasn't gold, it was people — his loved ones.

Suddenly Michael wanted to be home again. He pictured his mother and his father back at the cattle station. His father needed his help and he had let him down.

'What's going to happen now?' Kirsty said. 'We're not going to last long without water. Shall we keep going and see if we can find help?' They climbed aboard the Sail-Railer and crawled into the shade of the deckhouse.

'Well?' she persisted. 'What'll we do?'

'We could ask,' he said.

'Who?'

'You know.'

'Go on then.'

'Close your eyes.'

'You've changed,' she said. She closed her eyes.

Flies buzzed around the deckhouse, but they didn't distract him this time. 'Help us get home,' he said. 'Please.' He spoke the simple words in a voice filled with quiet assurance, the way Kirsty had spoken once before and it didn't ruin it a bit when he added: 'Please.'

Michael began to think more clearly. Pushing on to the end of the line, wherever that might lead them, seemed futile now.

'I'm tired of drifting along with the wind,' he said to Kirsty, opening his eyes. 'Enough. I reckon it's time to stop and think about the mess we're in. We can't go on. The prospector may come back; who knows? We can't just leave him. It's better to stay with the Sail-Railer and wait for help.'

But what about water? Kirsty did not ask the question, but the look in her eyes said it clearly.

He looked up at the mast with the sail furled at the top. The sail with the cross of stitches had brought them here. The sail had harnessed the power of the wind and carried them this far. If only it could help them now.

Perhaps it could. He told Kirsty about his plan.

When it grew cooler, they scratched out a large, shallow depression in the ground, using the skillet frying pan to dig with, and then they spread out the groundsheet like a shallow dish.

'We're doing what the camel lady said.'

'That's right, we're making a dew trap.'

They collected smooth stones that would help collect dew as well as weigh the sheet down and stop it from blowing away. They put the stones on the sheet. Michael took care to pucker up the stitched part of the sail, where Kirsty had sewn the cross, so that moisture would not leak through the needle holes.

When they had finished, the large groundsheet formed a giant collection dish. With a dish that size, they should drink very well by the morning, Michael thought wishfully.

His throat felt as if it had closed up, sealed with glue paste. It longed to feel the cool, parting slither of water down its length. In the morning, with luck, they would have water to drink — if they could last the night. They crawled back into the deckhouse and spent the rest of the day waiting.

'We must keep watch. Look out for planes. If we see one, we must wave and jump up and down and try to get their attention.'

Darkness came.

Thirst buzzed in their throats.

Michael imagined tiny droplets of dew forming on the surface of the groundsheet. He willed the little droplets to grow and run to join others, then to stream in silver rivulets into the hollows of the sheet ready to be collected in the bottle the next morning.

He imagined the musical tinkle of the water as he allowed it to trickle into the bottle. It turned into a waterfall in his mind — fresh, clear, blue-grey water filling the bottle to the brim, quivering on the brim then spilling over the top.

He imagined pools of it lying out there on the groundsheet.

Be patient. Wait till the morning.

They did not feel like talking with their throats burning. He discovered that severe thirst was more than a longing. It was physical pain, like a roaring sore throat. He felt shivery as if he were running a temperature. Too much sun. He had been exposed while he worked.

Perhaps it was the thirst and the shivery dreams that brought the panic.

He heard a far-off scouring and along with it the words of the camel lady's poem. He heard her speaking the words. . .

Her whistle shriek, her clanking rush,
The hiss of an iron sigh;
She'll ride again on her long lost tracks,
Just as in days gone by.

Her smoke once joined the horizon's span,
As she scribbled across the chart,
Writing the legend of the Ghan,
Across territory of the heart.

Where rail tracks meet on the red horizon,
I'll find the old Ghan train.
Where rail tracks meet on the red horizon,
I'll see her ride again.

He could hear something coming with a rushing sound.

The Sail-Railer trembled with the approach of something on the tracks. It was coming fast and gaining speed. He could hear the scribbling scurry of its rush.

The Ghost Ghan was coming!

13
An end to drifting

A PIERCING STEAM WHISTLE split the air. Michael snapped a look at the reclining form of Kirsty in the dark. She was still asleep. Why couldn't she hear it?

The Ghan was going to crash into the Sail-Railer at full speed, tonnes of steaming power boring along the track. He lifted his head to look for it, but he could see nothing, even though the sound came from straight ahead.

Nothing. A dream.

But the sound became a roar and kept coming. Then a shape grew in the darkness. It wasn't a steam train. It was a train of steam — not solid mass, but shape formed out of streaming vapour and moonlight, a steam demon blasting towards them. It was too late to move, even if he could. Fascination pinned him to the deck of the Sail-Railer.

> *Where rail tracks meet on the red horizon,*
> *I'll find the old Ghan train.*
> *Between the lines of infinity,*
> *I'll see her run again.*

She was running heedlessly towards them. Michael tried to call out a warning to Kirsty. But his throat sealed; the words stuck. He braced himself for the crash.

The apparition went through him like a chill, roaring wave, forcing its way into ears, eyes and throat — and deeper, through his skin and between the atoms of his body. The steam whistle screamed. He was a tunnel and the train was rushing through him — and miraculously he was still alive watching it go through him.

It threatened to take him with it, but Michael resisted. Let it go, he thought.

Then it was gone and there was not even the thinning roar of its going. It ran into a wall of silence.

Michael slept again, but the passing of the train seemed to have heated his body more and he shivered in a feverish way.

Michael sat up on the Sail-Railer at first light.

He saw a kangaroo nearby. It was perched on its back legs like a circus-trained animal. A giant rodent. Big, grey creature with twitching nose and ears, sharp claws and powerful tail curved out behind it like a playground slippery-dip. He wondered sleepily what had drawn it there. Was it looking for something? Water. Michael's thoughts took a swift turn of panic.

The 'roo was sitting beside their groundsheet.

Had it stolen their water? He jumped off the deck to the trackside.

'Go,' he said in a voice that croaked with dryness.

The kangaroo bounded off, with a parting glance of resentment. Michael discovered the tracks of the animal in the ground around the groundsheet, but it hadn't taken their water, or at least not all of it. There were still small pools of liquid glinting on the sheet.

'Sorry, old mate, it's ours,' he said to the parting kangaroo.

'What's wrong, Michael?' Kirsty said in a creaky voice.

"Roo tried to thieve our water.'

Their empty bottle lay on the sand beside the

groundsheet. Very carefully, fearing that he might lose a drop of their precious harvest, Michael removed the stones and lifted one corner of the groundsheet at a time, making the pools of water run together. He worked his way around the groundsheet until he had gathered all the pools in one section. Then he made a funnel to the edge and gathered up the rest of the groundsheet under his arm like bagpipes to squeeze the liquid into the neck of the bottle. In his eagerness, a few drops splashed over his hand. Slowly. Don't be too eager.

The liquid ran into the bottle and tinkled gloriously inside.

He squashed the groundsheet to squeeze out the last unwilling drops. There, it was all safely in the bottle. He hefted the bottle to judge how much he had collected. Half a bottle, maybe more. He had expected it to be heavy with water. He shook it. Water swished inside the bottle. Not a lot, not even a full bottle, but he had made water out of the desert, enough water to provide a few big mouthfuls for both of them, enough to split the claggy dryness of their throats.

He hurried with the bottle to Kirsty and gave it to her first. She sat up on one elbow, put it eagerly to her lips and gulped a mouthful down. Life seemed to flood back into her eyes. She cried, but there were no tears.

'Don't cry,' he said. 'That's moisture.'

Then it was Michael's turn. He put the mouth of the bottle to his lips and tipped it. A dash of blessed liquid forced its way through the gluey lining of his throat and, like the steam demon of his dreams, forced its way between the atoms of his body, but this time it was not a hostile invader. It was life, flooding back into him. He kept a small mouthful for later.

He joined Kirsty in the deckhouse. They breakfasted on the last of the shortbread. There was still a can of spaghetti and tomato sauce and a packet of water crackers. Kirsty shook her head at the sight of the water crackers. The name on the packet of biscuits was a cruel joke. Water crackers! They were drier than sand. If only they were real water.

But they could make their own water he had discovered and, if they were careful, very careful, they could stretch it out for a day or two.

No help came that day. No aeroplane passed overhead. Perhaps they weren't on a flight route, he worried. Could they be seen from the air? To improve their chances of being seen from the air, they made a landmark, using a stick to scratch the word *help* in the ground in giant letters. The effort, and the heat of the sun, sent them reeling back to the deckhouse for shelter.

The heat of the day had a sound like waves in Michael's ears, rumbling like a low roar on the shores of his senses. They lay, stunned, in the deckhouse. Flies added to their suffering.

The prospector didn't come. Where was he? Michael had time to think about the prospector and about his own headlong flight into nowhere.

'Dreams can be selfish things and you should never follow them at the expense of others,' the camel lady had said. 'Nor should you do it lightly. It's one thing to follow your dream — and another to just blow along with it. This country can kill you if you aren't careful. Without water and shade you can die in just nine hours.'

He had followed an old abandoned line to adventure and had found nothing — except maybe disaster.

Would help come in time? Did he care?

Perhaps he should just close his eyes and sleep. He had drifted with the wind; now he would drift with the sun and, wrapped in its scorching arms, let it take him where it wanted.

Then into his mind floated a picture of the prospector kneeling at a mound in the bush in front of a stone cross. He had come to revisit his treasure, his loved ones.

Michael pictured his mother and father, sitting at dinner, looking at his empty chair. He turned to Kirsty who lay dozing. He couldn't give up.

That evening, like fishermen spreading a net, they spread their dew trap again, hoping to catch a rich haul of condensation.

There were no nightmares and no ghost trains that night. Michael and Kirsty slept heavily.

The sound of an engine in the sky woke Michael. It was morning. A plane was coming. He nudged Kirsty awake. 'Plane — maybe it's looking for us.'

They spilled off the trolley and craned their necks, hunting the sky. It was a twin-engined light aircraft, flying at a fairly high altitude. Could it see them from up there?

Kirsty jumped up and down and waved. 'Here we are – can't you see us?' she shouted in a voice as cracked as the dry earth she jumped on.

The plane was too high, Michael thought, tasting despair.

But this might be their last chance.

They needed to make a clearly visible signal. Michael looked around for something to wave. His eye fell on the orange groundsheet. Without hesitation, he grabbed one corner and pulled it up. It was damp with dew and crackled stiffly like lettuce in his hands. The stones flew off the sheet. Water sprayed off it. He spun, with the groundsheet making a flapping orange circle in the air for the pilot to see.

The plane pointed its nose disdainfully towards the horizon.

'Are you blind?' he shouted.

'No good, Michael.'

Michael dropped the groundsheet away in disgust. The plane had brought a surge of hope, and now disappointment. It had also brought disaster.

'I've lost our water.'

Michael picked up the groundsheet. It was still damp and dewy. He gave it to Kirsty. 'You can lick off the moisture. You have it. It was my stupid fault.'

Kirsty licked some of the remaining specks of dew off the groundsheet and tears came to her eyes, but this time they were tears of disappointment.

Michael felt like crying, too, but his eyes were too dry.

She left him half of the groundsheet. The moisture wet his lips and amounted to a mouthful, no more.

'We're going to die out here,' Kirsty said.

'If we do, it'll be my fault.'

'No it won't. I wanted to go with you. Dreams are easy to get swept along with — even other people's, especially when they're as sure of them as you were.'

'I was dumb, dumb, dumb.'

'No you weren't. It's been a great adventure. Nothing like this happens at home.'

'If we do get out of here and you go back to England, would you ever come back to Australia?'

She smiled as brightly as she could through dry lips. 'What do you think? You know you can't get rid of me.'

The sun was at its height in the sky.

They came silently on carefully placed, padded feet, in a long-necked swaying gait – archly amused-looking creatures, three tied together; and on the first rode an old woman in a bush hat with long hair that fell around her shoulders like a grey tent.

She made a whooshing sound to the camel she rode and, with long-limbed grace, it collapsed to the sand in stages, first with one knee lowered to the ground, then the other, then the hind legs before the forelimbs were settled, and it settled its entire weight on its breast pad.

The old woman dismounted. 'It's a little dry for you, ducks,' she said. 'I've come to take you home.'

'We can't go home yet. The prospector's out there. We must find him.'

'You won't find him. Not here. Only in the pages of a history book. I remembered seeing his face. That's why I came back. We've both been travelling with a ghost, me with the Ghost Ghan and you with the ghost of a man.'

She brought them a bottle of water and let them drink freely. Kirsty cried in relief.

'Your parents aren't going to believe this — or me, are they, ducks? They'll think that I'm a crazed old woman and that you're a pair of crazy young people. And they'd be right. But it's time to go home. I have two spare camels waiting for you, so let's make a start.'

They rode away on the camels, creatures with skin as rough as coconut husks. Michael and Kirsty turned a farewell glance at the Sail-Railer.

The bright sun played a trick, bleaching out all signs of the railway tracks. It appeared as if the Sail-Railer sat stranded on bare ground.

'Goodbye, Willy-Willy Express,' Kirsty said.

Michael turned his face towards home.

14

Camel route

IT SEEMED PERFECTLY RIGHT to be going back by camel, he thought, looking over the head of the animal.

They were going back in time, travelling the path of the oldest Ghan trains of all, the camel trains that followed the camel route known as the Ghan Track. Once, before the track was finished in 1929, when many of the camels were set free, there had been 20 000 camels carrying supplies and equipment into Australia, the camel lady told them.

They had gone from one ship of the desert to another.

Michael's camel was named Delilah and the creature's coconut-husk head rose on a long, impossibly thin neck from its broad body, like the stem post of an antique Viking ship.

The camel lady said that her camels could carry half a tonne of load — some bulls had even been known to lift a full tonne and it was not unknown for a camel to travel over a hundred kilometres a day if pushed.

Delilah was loaded with drums of water and an assortment of canvas and leather bags that were enough to break the axle of a pick-up truck, Michael thought. They travelled in a train, the camel lady in front, riding on Alice, and the other camels linked by nose lines and halter ropes. Michael's saddle was so broad that it made his hip joints ache and made him afraid that he would split, but it did not seem to bother the camel lady or Kirsty. When Delilah turned her head, Michael was surprised by her sweep of glamorous eyelashes.

They rode for a few hours and then dismounted and walked to stretch their legs. They camped at night and sat around a fire under the stars and the camel lady cooked them food over the fire. Afterwards she produced two spare bedrolls for them to sleep in.

Early in the morning they set out again, and travelled until just before noon. They rested in the shade of some acacias until four o'clock, then travelled again until eight or nine.

The journey was as timeless as the land they

passed through and Michael grew used to the feeling of the saddle. The swaying gait of the camel lulled him into memories of their trip and made him think about what had happened to them and what should happen when he finally reached home.

There would be trouble from his father and mother. That was unavoidable and a part of himself did not want to avoid it. He had to face up to the consequences of drifting away with his dreams. It seemed perfectly right.

The camel lady took them all the way to the place where the two ghost gums stood like sentinels and the tracks ended like the prongs of a fork sticking out over the edge of a table.

'Goodbye, ducks — back to the real world for you,' she said, waving a cheery farewell.

They watched her leave and then started to walk along the side of the tracks.

Out of the heat, the stringy, dark figure of Maralinga Jim came trudging beside the tracks to meet them. 'Where you kids been?' he said. 'Michael, your father bin lookin' for you.'

'The willy-willy came,' Michael said, apologetically.

Maralinga's deep-set eyes squinted over their shoulders and they twisted to follow his line of vision. In the distance they saw the Sail-Railer sitting on a bare stretch of ground, flung off her rails and stranded.

'I help you put this feller back on the track,' he said. 'Then I push you back alonga track. Your father bin lookin' for you long long time, maybe two hours.'

Two hours.

Had it been that long? Michael thought.